O9-ABI-762

$35.00   1/05

Chicago Public Library

REFERENCE

Form 178 rev. 11-00

CHICAGO PUBLIC LIBRARY
SOUTH CHICAGO BRANCH
9055 S. HOUSTON AVE. 60617

WEAPONS TECHNOLOGY

HISTORY OF INVENTION

WEAPONS TECHNOLOGY

Tim Ripley

CHICAGO PUBLIC LIBRARY
SOUTH CHICAGO BRANCH
9055 S. HOUSTON AVE. 60617

Facts On File, Inc.

Copyright © 2004 The Brown Reference Group plc.

All rights reserved. No part of this book may be reproduced or utilized in any form or by any means, electronic or mechanical, including photocopying, recording, or by any information storage or retrieval systems, without permission in writing from the publisher. For information contact:

Facts On File, Inc.
132 West 31st Street
New York, NY 10001

Library of Congress Cataloging-in-Publication Data

Ripley, Tim
    Weapons technology / Tim Ripley.
      p. cm.
      Summary: Introduces the development of weapon technology, from the dawn of civilization to the present, including slings and arrows, attack submarines, and nuclear bombs.
    Includes bibliographical references and index.
    ISBN 0-8160-5438-X
    1. Weapons—Juvenile literature. 2. Military art and science—Juvenile literature.
[1. Weapons—History. 2. Military art and science—History.] I. Title.

U800.R57 2004
623.4—dc22

2003013444

Facts On File books are available at special discounts when purchased in bulk quantities for businesses, associations, institutions, or sales promotions. Please call our Special Sales Department in New York at (212) 967-8800 or (800) 322-8755.

You can find Facts On File on the World Wide Web at http://www.factsonfile.com

For The Brown Reference Group plc:
Project Editor: Tom Jackson
Design: Bradbury and Williams
Picture Research: Becky Cox
Managing Editor: Bridget Giles
Consultant: Dr. Fletcher M. Lamkin, President,
    Westminster College, Fulton, Missouri.

Printed and bound in Singapore

10 9 8 7 6 5 4 3 2 1

The acknowledgments on page 96 form part of this copyright page. Every effort has been made to contact copyright holders of any material reproduced in this book. Any omission will be rectified in subsequent printings if notice is given to the publishers.

CONTENTS

$35.00

R03027 93929

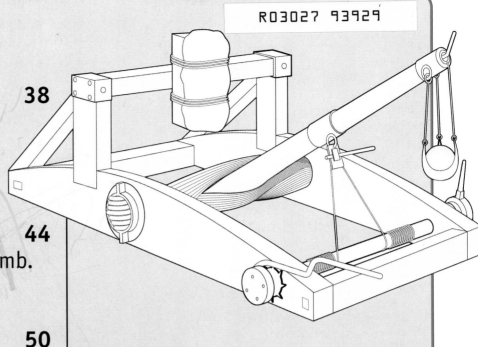

PREHISTORIC WEAPONS

Warfare is as old as civilization itself. In prehistoric times, people began using primitive stone and wooden tools, such as hand-axes and clubs, as weapons. As they do still, rival individuals or gangs fought and killed each other to settle disagreements. The first wars were probably waged between neighboring villages. As is often the case today, people battled over territory and resources, such as water and food supplies.

METALWORKING

It took the development of early civilizations and city-states in Mesopotamia and Egypt between 3500 and 3000 B.C.E. for warfare

as we know it today to evolve. As these societies developed on the banks of the Euphrates, Tigris, and Nile Rivers, they began to form armies to protect their cities and wealth from attack.

The key advance in technology in this period was the invention of metalwork to create household implements and jewelry. Copper was the first metal to be used, and it was soon being crafted into swords and dagger blades, armor, and sharp, pointed heads for spears and arrows.

Societies that could make metal weapons were able to defeat and conquer those still relying on primitive stone ones. This early

A stone carving made in Iraq 4,500 years ago shows soldiers marching into battle. They have metal helmets and are carrying shields and long spears. The spears' pointed metal heads are tied to wooden handles.

A 4,000-year-old bronze blade (right) and the stone used to sharpen it (left). The green color on the rock and blade is caused by copper metal reacting with the air.

warfare was unforgiving, with all trace of the losing side being erased as its people were either killed or enslaved.

A thousand years through history, metalworkers found out how to harden copper by mixing it with another metal, tin, to create bronze. Copper armor and sword blades shattered when struck by weapons made of bronze, and this new alloy (mixture of metals) gave a huge advantage in battle. The Indus Valley civilization, in what is now part of India and Pakistan, grew due to the strength of bronze weapons. By 2000 B.C.E. iron, an even tougher metal, began to replace bronze. New civilizations armed with superior iron weapons, such as the Hittites of eastern Turkey, began to conquer huge empires.

Key inventions

Arrowheads

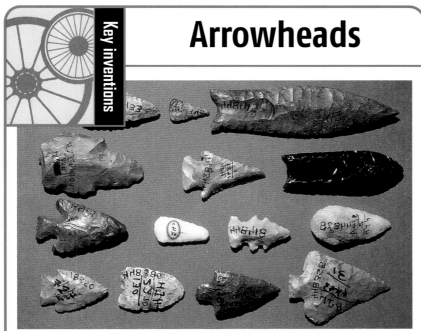

Bows and arrows have been in use for about 7,000 years. They were originally used for hunting animals but were soon adopted as an effective long-range weapon. At first, arrows were tipped with heads (above) made from hard but brittle materials, such as bone, stone, and natural glass. Heads of bronze and iron gave arrows a much greater penetrative power.

Native American fighters began using arrows 1,500 years ago, having fought and hunted with stone-headed spears before then. Until European traders supplied them with iron arrowheads, most arrows were tipped with a stone called flint. Flint breaks naturally into sharp pieces. Stone arrowheads are sharpened by using a bone tool that flakes off thin chips.

ORGANIZED FIGHTERS

Soldiers of the first organized military forces, or armies went into battle armed with a wide range of weapons. Swords and daggers were the main weapons for killing hand-to-hand. Long pikes were also used to kill an opponent before he could get close enough to use his sword. Spears and shorter javelins were thrown to strike at the enemy from farther away. Another advance in battlefield technology was cavalry. Soldiers rode into battle on a horse or elephant. They moved faster than soldiers on foot and charged through the enemy, breaking up its defenses.

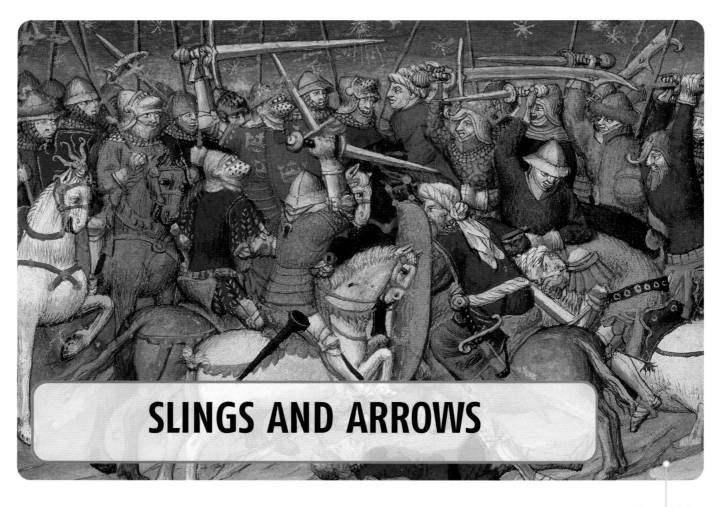

SLINGS AND ARROWS

Warfare in the ancient world saw the development of sophisticated tactics and complex armies. For several thousand years until firearms began to be used on the battlefield in the 14th century, the sword, spear, pike, and bow were the tools of war.

While weapons technology was moving forward at a slow pace, success in battle generally depended on the efficiency and discipline of the fighting force and careful, strategic planning. Huge empires—from Egypt to Byzantium—all rose and fell as their military systems were eventually defeated by opponents armed with new and superior weapons.

COMMAND STRUCTURE

Today, armed forces are very professional organizations controlled by a clear command structure, from the basic soldier to the commander-in-chief. This modern system is relatively new. For thousands of years, fighting men were led into battle by a king or noble leaders. But warfare was more than just a matter of two groups of armed men fighting it out to the death. Whole societies had to be mobilized to support their ruler's war effort. Taxes were used to buy weapons, pay soldiers, and build military bases. Armies were increasingly grouped into specific units. These units were either based on their

A painting of the battle between the army of Alexander the Great and the forces of Indian king Porus in 334 B.C.E. Battles in this period were generally chaotic. Once the armies came together, soldiers fought hand-to-hand.

8

member's skills—infantry, cavalry, and archers, for example—or loyalty to a particular commander or region of the kingdom.

Victory against such an organized army depended on soldiers being disciplined and trained to a high degree, so they could perform complex maneuvers on the battlefield. Armies began to wear uniforms and carry flags so that the generals could follow the progress of their troops from a vantage point. Musical instruments such as trumpets, bugles, and drums were used to pass orders to soldiers over the noise of battle.

LAND AND SEA

The empires of the ancient era stretched across continents, and armies needed long supply chains to defend the territory effectively. Controlling the sea was just as vital as commanding the land. The first warships were galleys rowed by slaves. They cruised the Mediterranean Sea and along ocean coastlines. Several times in history the future of an empire or state was decided by action taking place at sea.

The ancient Greek city-states were some of the first societies to focus themselves on military activity, to prevent invasion by their neighbors. Athens and Sparta became the most powerful and famous Greek city-states because of their pioneering military systems. Their forces repeatedly defeated more numerous enemies by using a highly disciplined formation of infantry soldiers known as the *phalanx*.

Soldiers in a phalanx were protected by heavy armor and equipped with sturdy 10-foot (3-m) pikes. They formed solid rectangles up to 50 men deep with pikes protruding on all sides. The phalanx was a defensive formation, even able to hold out against attack from mounted soldiers. Although phalanxes were sometimes used to attack the enemy, soldiers forming a phalanx

Key inventions

Chariots

Rulers first went into battle on horse-drawn chariots so their armies could spot them in the chaos, but these vehicles soon came into their own as effective weapons. The Hyksos, an ancient civilization that existed in modern-day Palestine 3,500 years ago, were the first to use chariots in battle. The Hyksos, who strengthened wheels with iron, used chariots to conquer Egypt.

Other societies began to use chariots. They proved to be useful for breaking through infantry ranks, especially when blades were attached to the wheels (above, an 11th-century Mongol chariot). However, chariots could only be used in open and flat country. Charioteers became vulnerable if their vehicles were damaged or horses injured during a raid through enemy territory.

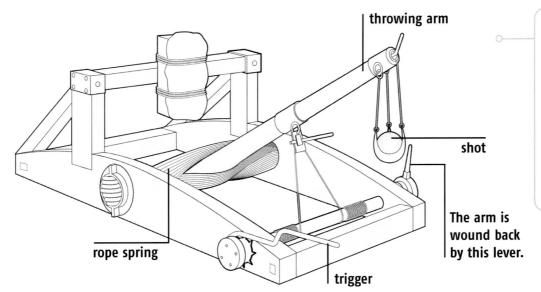

throwing arm

shot

The arm is wound back by this lever.

rope spring

trigger

A Roman catapult called an onager, meaning "wild ass." The weapon earned this name because of its recoil kick. The stone shot was flung forward by a spring made from a coiled rope.

could not move forward in close formation very quickly and would break up crossing rough ground.

Offensive moves were generally started by archers, javelin throwers, or men armed with slingshots, who were positioned behind or at the side of the phalanx. Their missiles would soften up enemy defenses before the phalanx's shock troops began to advance. Alexander the Great of Macedonia used soldiers in these formations to carve out a huge empire from Egypt to India about 330 B.C.E.

RISE AND FALL
By the first century C.E., the Romans, the most powerful military power to date, had taken control of the Mediterranean region. The Romans were able to conquer most of western Europe, North Africa, and the Middle East thanks to their system of legions. These were self-contained fighting units set up to operate far from the Roman homeland in present-day Italy. Every legion had field

engineers who designed fortified camps, fully equipped with drains and food stores. A legion—up to 6,000 men—could build a temporary camp in a few hours, even after a day of marching.

History enthusiasts dress up as Roman legionaries. They are armed with a javelin, short sword, and a curved shield.

Samurai Sword

A samurai's sword (left) is made of steel (a mixture of iron, carbon and, in this case, silicon) and is one of the sharpest and strongest of any traditional sword. Each one is made by hand by a highly skilled swordmaker.

The swordmaker introduces carbon and silicon to the iron by covering it in clay and ash before it is heated. Once the steel reaches the correct mixture, it is bent over on itself several times, heated to an exact temperature, and hammered flat. This process creates many tough and hardened layers within the blade. The swordmaker would judge when the heated blade reached the critical temperature by looking at the color of the metal in the furnace. This phase of the process was generally done in the dark of night when it is easier to see the color more precisely.

For much of medieval history, Japan was ravaged by conflicts between rival noblemen, or *samurai*, who battled for the right to rule as the *Shogun*. Like European knights, Japanese samurai considered individual combat highly honorable. They equipped themselves with two curved swords.

Instead of unwieldy pikes, a Roman soldier carried a javelin (short spear), a short sword, and a light shield. These armaments allowed formations of Roman soldiers to move rapidly around the battlefield, performing surprise moves to hit enemies from unexpected directions. Legions were frequently drilled to practice formation changes without exposing gaps in their ranks. They were also skilled at creating shield walls to provide protection from enemy arrows.

The professional Roman soldiers relentlessly wore down less organized and motivated opponents. Rome's military dominance lasted into the fifth century, when the city of Rome itself was ransacked by so-called "barbarian" armies—the Vandals, Huns, Ostrogoths, and Visigoths.

These invading tribes came from northern and eastern Europe. They revolutionized the use of cavalry, fielding huge armies made up almost exclusively of mounted soldiers. Fast-moving light cavalry armed with bows and slingshots provided fire support for more heavily armored horsemen, who rode through the enemy ranks cutting down foot soldiers.

Viking raiders from Scandinavia pioneered the use of longships to mount seaborne invasions of enemy territory. Their fierce raiding parties terrorized the coasts of Europe for centuries.

EAST AND WEST

While Greece and Rome dominated the political map of ancient Europe, they were by no means the world leaders in weapons technology. Empires in China and India also had hugely powerful armies, in many ways more advanced than those of Europe. In general, these Asian societies were less interested than the cultures to the west in contacting foreigners. (*Continued on page 14.*)

SIEGE ENGINES

Sieges have always been an important tactic in warfare, even today. However, modern sieges are a lot less brutal than those of the past, when defeated armies retreated into castles or behind fortified city walls to prevent advancing enemy troops from getting within stabbing distance. In response, an attacking army would seal off their enemy's refuge, denying them food or water in the hope that the weakened defenders would surrender or be easier to defeat in a final assault.

The ancient Greeks built siege machines, or engines, to break into fortifications. Sieges lasted many weeks or months, and armies did not generally bring their siege engines with them, but built them from raw materials found in the local region while the siege continued.

Siege engines had two functions—to either get weapons and troops over the wall, or to go through it. Huge wooden catapults were used to throw rocks at fortifications to damage walls and kill defenders on the ramparts. During prolonged sieges, catapults were also used to throw carcasses of

A scene from a siege during the Crusades in the 11th century. The attacking forces are using catapults to bombard the walls. At the bottom of the picture (A) attackers are preparing to cross the moat inside a covered siege engine (B). In the center of the picture, a siege tower is being moved into position. The tower has a covering of animal skins to protect the people inside from arrows. Meanwhile, the defenders are also using catapults positioned in the towers (C). They are attempting to set the siege engine on fire with firebrands (burning arrows).

dead animals into besieged cities in attempts to pollute water supplies and spread disease among the defenders. Gates were battered down by rams protected by armored roofs. To assault city walls, wheeled siege ladders, or *sambucas*, were rolled up to them to create a platform for troops to launch an attack.

Siege engines took several days to construct and often required several weeks to complete. Armies of laborers, usually prisoners or slaves, were used to build and then push them into action. These laborers were also put to work digging trenches and building embankments to protect the siege engines. This was a very dangerous job since the workers were in view of the enemy. The laborers were also set to work building ramps made of earth up against the fortifications. Assault troops would use the ramps in attempts to storm the walls.

It was very rare for defenders to just wait and allow siege engines to be brought into action. They often mounted raids against the enemy and prepared their defenses for when the siege engines were put into use. They dropped heavy rocks and "Greek fire"—a flaming mixture of tar, resin, sulfur, and coals—from the ramparts onto battering rams or hurled them at approaching troops.

Sambuca

Battering Ram

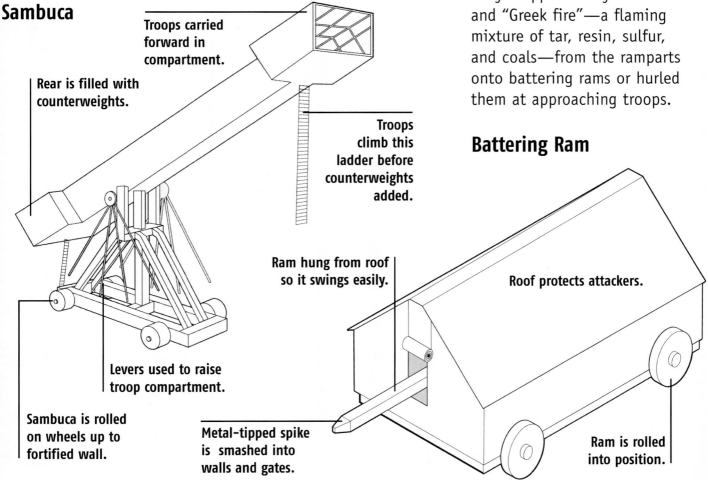

Sambuca

Rear is filled with counterweights.

Troops carried forward in compartment.

Troops climb this ladder before counterweights added.

Levers used to raise troop compartment.

Sambuca is rolled on wheels up to fortified wall.

Battering Ram

Ram hung from roof so it swings easily.

Roof protects attackers.

Metal-tipped spike is smashed into walls and gates.

Ram is rolled into position.

The Chinese developed many new technologies, including gunpowder, the first explosive. Many of these advances were first used for non-military purposes. Meanwhile, the powers of Europe and the Middle East were continually developing their weapons technologies.

LORD AND LAND

Medieval Europe saw the rise of feudal military systems. These involved a nobleman raising an army on behalf of his king. His force was a mix of small groups of highly trained knights and men-at-arms, supported by hordes of poorly armed amateur fighters, who were drawn from the population of peasant farmers who rented their land from noblemen.

The 13th and 14th centuries saw Europe ravaged by a series of savage wars, as royal houses struggled to seize power and land. Feudal armies proved unsuitable for long campaigns. The ordinary soldiers had to be released from service to tend to their crops for several months of the year, otherwise they would starve. It was also very difficult to train feudal soldiers beyond a basic level, which made complex tactics and battle plans difficult. Once a medieval army was launched into battle, it was very difficult to control, and soldiers were prone to panic if it suffered a setback.

The weaknesses of their armies forced European rulers to employ mercenaries (soldiers who fight for money), generally from Switzerland or Germany. These soldiers carried pikes and fought in phalanxes like the armies of ancient Greece.

To beat the threat posed by these well-drilled pikemen, French commanders formed units of *gendarmes*, who were professional cavalry soldiers. In response to these new forces, English armies began to rely on highly skilled archers, who used powerful longbows to shower the enemy with devastating bursts of high-speed arrows from long distance.

How things work

Composite Bow

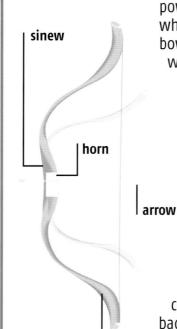

sinew

horn

arrow

reverse curve

The composite bow was a key weapon used by the horsemen of the Mongol Empire. Unlike other bows, the Mongols could use this small but powerful weapon to devastating effect while riding horses at high speed. The bow was made from flexible strips of wood glued together and bent into a reverse curve—a stronger shape than that of normal bows.

Animal sinew was bound to the front of the bow and a piece of horn was lashed to the back. When the archer pulled back on the bow, bending the wood, the sinew was stretched and the horn was compressed. Once the archer let go, the stretched sinew pulled, and the compressed horn pushed the bow back into its original shape very quickly, launching the arrow at a high speed. Only the English longbow could achieve similar speeds to the composite but was too long to be used on horseback.

Pikemen clash during a re-enactment of a English battle from 1642. The hugely long pikes were hard to wield in battle but they could injure the enemy from a long distance.

EASTERN ATTACKERS

Ghengis Khan (1162–1227) was a legendary military leader from Mongolia who conquered China in the 13th century and began to build a kingdom from Korea to Hungary—the largest land empire the world has ever known.

Ghengis Khan's hordes of fierce fighters were armed with composite bows and battled on horseback. The Mongol armies were successful mainly as a result of their vast numbers. Their fast-moving cavalrymen swept in waves through the flanks of enemy armies, which were made up mainly of foot soldiers. Those soldiers who managed to survive often retreated to fortified cities.

They were left at the mercy of the Mongols, who cut off their food and water supplies.

In the 15th century, Islamic armies from the Persian Gulf brought down Byzantium, the remains of the Roman Empire that stretched from southeast Europe to North Africa. The Islamic force was centered around the Ottoman Turks, whose sultans used light cavalry to control an empire from Spain to Iran. The Turks were great innovators in naval warfare, siege tactics, and early forms of artillery. In 1453, they used all these techniques to take Constantinople—the fortress capital of the Byzantine Empire, known today as Istanbul.

KNIGHTS

Knights were a central part of the military system in Europe's Middle Ages (400–1500 C.E.). In return for being allowed to rule over their own land by the monarch, knights and other nobles, such as lords and barons, had to provide troops whenever asked by the king.

Each nobleman was responsible for raising, arming, equipping, and feeding all the troops he commanded. In return, he received a percentage of any treasure or lands seized from the enemy during the war. Most nobles raised their forces from among the peasant farmers who lived on their land. When called to arms by the king, nobles led their troops into battle. Each fighting unit took its place in the battle line according to its leader's seniority.

Combat between medieval armies was governed by a strict code of chivalry, in which nobles treated each other differently than the peasant soldiers. Knights captured on the battlefield were treated more as honored guests than enemy prisoners of war by their captors. They were held for huge ransoms,

A medieval knight rallies his bodyguard around him.

16

Jousting

Knights who went into battle on horseback fought by jousting. This involved riding at high speed at an opponent, trying to hit him with a long lance. Knights practiced this skill at jousting tournaments.

1. This lance has a sharp blade. Those used in tournaments had blunt tips.

2. A helmet with a pointed visor deflects blows away from the face.

3. The knight wears metal armor, although this was too heavy for long battles.

4. The horse also wore a protective coat. The pattern on this coat identified a knight on the battlefield.

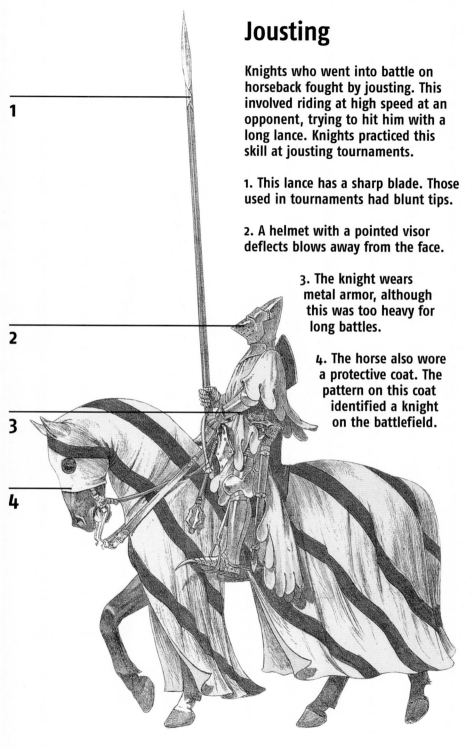

example, would have cost $150,000 today. Most nobles and their loyal companions went into battle wearing chain mail, metal helmets, shin pads, and arm pads. Full armored protection was often more trouble than it was worth because it was so hard to move around in.

While ordinary soldiers went into battle with little more than a pike, their leaders were armed with a collection of weapons. These included heavy swords, axes, mallets, and maces (spiked clubs), to maximize their killing potential at short range.

The usual way for medieval nobles to go into battle was on foot, in a formation known as a "combat." The senior noble would gather as many close relatives and loyal attendants as possible around him. They would form a bodyguard for their leader. The peasant soldiers would be deployed on either side or were sent out in front.

Once a combat closed with the enemy, the leaders of rival fighters would try to kill each other. If the leader was killed, the peasant soldiers would generally give up and flee. In the long term, the main strategic aim of a knight was to kill as many enemy nobles as possible. This aimed to reduce the number of people loyal to the enemy king.

while ordinary soldiers were generally put to death if they fell into enemy hands.

Although the popular image of a knight has him riding on a horse, only a few noblemen actually fought on horseback. Few horses could carry the full weight of a knight armored in metal for more than a couple of hours. The cost of horses, armor, and weaponry meant only the most wealthy of nobles could afford all the equipment. A 16th-century knight's equipment, for

SHOOTING WARS

Explosives were first used on a battlefield by the Chinese in 1161 during their war with the Mongols. The Chinese used gunpowder, which had been invented at least a century before, to make loud and threatening noises. They did not fire a missile at the enemy and were largely ineffective. However, within a few years, both Chinese and Indian armies were using rockets—little more than large fireworks—and bamboo mortars to bombard the enemy.

ARTILLERY
At first gunpowder was just known as black powder, since guns had not been invented.

Knowledge of the powder arrived in Europe in the 13th century, through contact with Mongols.

English philosopher Roger Bacon and the German monk Berthold Schwarz studied

Using guns in battles caused devastation, as this painting of French troops taking a Russian stronghold at the end of the Crimean War in 1855 shows.

An English gunner lights the fuse of a primitive cannon used at the Battle of Crécy in 1346. The cannon could be fitted with two widths of barrel. The wider one is on the ground.

gunpowder and were among the first to develop it into a faster-burning explosive that could be used to fire heavy missiles from cannons. The English were the first to use cannons in combat, during the Battle of Crécy against the French in 1346. The new weapons, however, had little influence on the outcome of the battle. Instead it was the English archers who won the fight. These highly mobile foot soldiers used powerful longbows to inflict heavy casualties on the well-armored but slow mounted French troops.

The first cannons were little more than metal tubes open at one end. Cannonballs made of iron and stone were loaded through the opening and packed into the closed end along with

Gunpowder

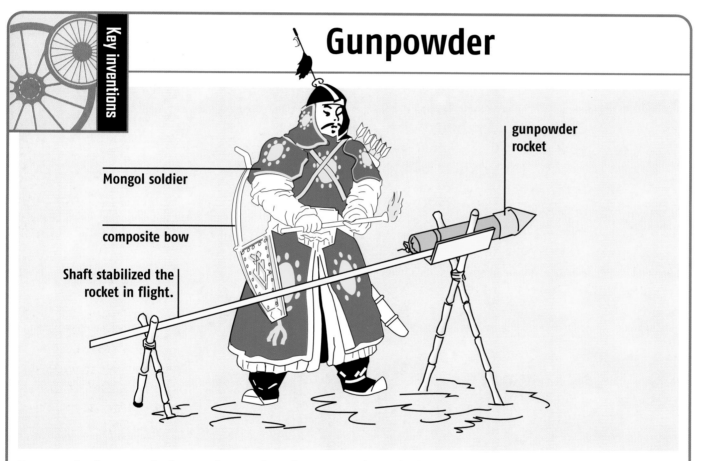

Key inventions

gunpowder rocket

Mongol soldier

composite bow

Shaft stabilized the rocket in flight.

Gunpowder is an explosive made up of a mixture of powdered substances. The black powder first used in warfare contained saltpeter (potassium nitrate), charcoal, and sulfur. When the powder is set on fire, the constituents react together and release hot gases. The explosive force is created by these gases expanding rapidly. When directed through a small hole, like a firework nozzle such as of a war rocket (above), the explosion shoots the rocket forward. If the explosion is directed through the barrel of a gun, it pushes bullets or cannonballs out with it at high speed. The sulfur in black powder corrodes the metal in the gun barrels, and black powder also produces a lot of soot and smoke. The powder used in guns today is smokeless gunpowder. This contains nitrocellulose, which goes off when it is hit and does not need to be set alight. The first smokeless explosive was *guncotton*, so called because it is made from cotton soaked in nitric acid.

gunpowder. The gunpowder was ignited by a red-hot iron poked through a small hole. As it exploded, the cannonball was flung out of the open end. Early cannons were very inaccurate. They were used to fire small pellets into soldiers or to propel larger balls at fortified walls.

DECISIVE WEAPONS

By the 15th century, most armies in Europe and Asia were using artillery, both heavy siege guns and more mobile cannons for use on the battlefield. Advances in metal casting made barrels much stronger, while improvements made gunpowder more reliable.

The Turks had shown the potential of artillery in siege warfare when they used 70 guns to blast holes in the mighty defenses of Constantinople in 1453. At the same time, the Bureau brothers, three French generals, were developing revolutionary cannons that could smash through the walls of castles in just a few days. These mighty guns made massive castles, with their thick stone walls, obsolete, and people began to rethink the designs of their fortifications. The French army were also the first to use light artillery guns against troops on the battlefield. These guns were towed into battle on horse-drawn carriages. Their barrels were mounted on pivots so the gunners could raise and lower their weapon to aim it at targets at different ranges.

HANDGUNS

Toward the end of the 15th century, firearms began to replace blades as a soldier's main weapon. Early handguns were called hand cannons or fire sticks. They were small versions of large artillery cannons made from iron or brass that could be held and aimed by a soldier. They did not fire bullets as we know them today but small cannonballs. These primitive firearms were very heavy and inaccurate. They got so hot after being fired that they could not be reloaded for several minutes.

The matchlock firing mechanism made handguns easier to use. Matchlock weapons used a fuse soaked in saltpeter to ignite a pan of gunpowder on the top of the weapon. The flash in the pan

The advances in artillery forced fortifications to be redesigned to protect against cannonballs. The French engineer Sebastian Vauban revolutionized the design of fortresses by introducing huge earthwork ramparts (below) that were designed to absorb cannonballs.

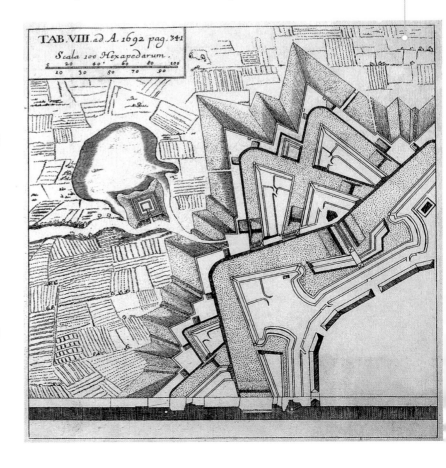

exploded gunpowder packed inside the barrel, forcing the bullet out of the other end.

FIRING MECHANISMS

Unlike earlier firearms, the barrels of matchlocks were set in a stock made from wood. This made them easier to handle when hot. The wooded stock was often hooked so the gun could be held at the shoulder when being fired, making it reasonably accurate up to 320 feet (100 meters). Matchlocks were still not ideal weapons since they weighed between 15 and 25 pounds (6 to 12 kg), so the soldier had to rest the weapon on a fork to be able to fire.

When fired together in volleys, several matchlocks could produce devastating firepower, but they took a long time to reload. Gunpowder and shot had to be dropped into the muzzle (barrel opening) and packed down with a ramrod before the fuse could be lit. Soldiers armed with guns (musketeers) were vulnerable to cavalry attack while trying to reload. Armies used squads of pikemen to protect their gunmen.

It took the introduction of bayonets in the late 17th century to finally see the demise of the pike from European battlefields. Plug bayonets—blades that fitted into the gun barrel—had been developed earlier in the century, but the weapon could not fire when the bayonet was plugged into the barrel. In 1680, the first ring bayonets, which fitted around the muzzle of a musket appeared, and within a couple of decades the pike was obsolete.

FIELD OF FIRE

The bayonet led to a century of "horse and musket" warfare, which culminated in the defeat of the French emperor Napoleon

Instructions from Holland in 1637 show the many steps needed to load, fire, and transport a musket effectively.

practifed in the warres of the united Nether-lands.   19

1. Reft your Mufket.
2. Drawe out your match.
3. Blowe your match.
4. Cock your match.
5. Try your match
6. Gard your panne.
7. Prefent
8. Giue fire.
9. Come vp to yo' mufket.
10. Returne your match.
11. Take vp your rest.
12. Blowe of your loose powder & Cast about your mufket.
13. Traile your rest & open your charge &c.
14. Bringe vp your musket
15. Poize yo' mufket and recouuer your rest.
16. Shoulder your mufket.

Firing Mechanisms

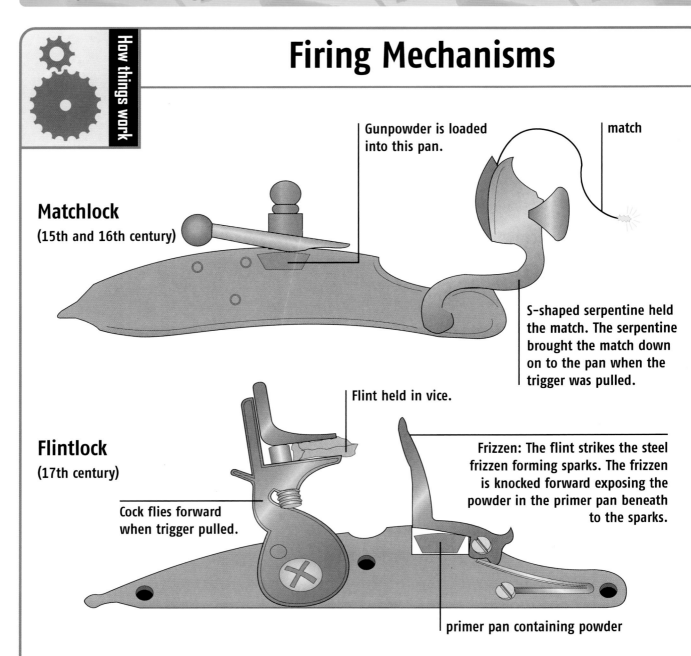

Gunpowder is loaded into this pan.

match

Matchlock
(15th and 16th century)

S-shaped serpentine held the match. The serpentine brought the match down on to the pan when the trigger was pulled.

Flint held in vice.

Flintlock
(17th century)

Frizzen: The flint strikes the steel frizzen forming sparks. The frizzen is knocked forward exposing the powder in the primer pan beneath to the sparks.

Cock flies forward when trigger pulled.

primer pan containing powder

The flintlock and matchlock muskets were notoriously unreliable. The powder in the primer pan often failed to ignite the charge inside the barrel, and the muskets were almost useless in rain because wet powder cannot burn. These problems were solved by the percussion cap, invented by Scottish gunsmith Alexander Forsyth in 1807. Instead of filling a pan, the priming powder was enclosed in a small cylindrical cap. The cap was placed into a tube that led into the barrel. When the trigger was pulled, a cocked hammer swung down on to the cap sending an explosion into the barrel, igniting the main charge, and firing the shot. Although percussion-lock weapons were still loaded by packing shot and powder through the muzzle, they were the transition between flintlocks and more modern firing mechanisms. Modern bullets, which were invented later in the 19th century, incorporated the primer charge and bullet into a single unit, or cartridge, that is loaded through the side of the barrel.

Fact A blunderbus is a musket with a bell-shaped muzzle. It fired many small pellets at once, called buckshot. The name *blunderbus* means "thunder-gun."

Bonaparte (1769–1821) by British and German forces at Waterloo in 1815. European armies became very disciplined forces that were trained to maintain formations and handle their weapons under pressure. Ranks of hundreds of soldiers could deliver repeated volleys of bullets over long periods of time. By that time troops were using flintlock firearms, which used sparks to ignite their charges. Flintlocks were easier to load and less likely to misfire than matchlocks. A regiment of infantry could fire up to 500 rounds a minute, sweeping the area 480 feet (150 meters) in front of them with deadly fire.

Infantry forces used volleys of fire as their main tactic. Soldiers who fired alone at individual targets were taking a big risk because their muskets were very hard to aim. By standing together in long lines and firing in volleys, infantry regiments were able to bring heavy firepower to bear on

targets. A regiment would be arranged in two ranks of soldiers for battle. Once the front-rank troops had fired they would reload, while those in the second rank aimed and fired. The first rank would then be ready to fire again and the process would be repeated. A volley of musket fire of this kind could inflict huge losses at close range, and made it almost impossible for even a high-speed cavalry charge to get near enough to attack.

When field artillery guns became light enough to be moved around the battlefield quickly, they were used to support infantry fire. When artillery was targeted at soldiers it could devastate infantry ranks. Cannonballs could rip through several ranks of troops from many hundreds of feet away, and, at closer range, canisters of small shot were fired to create a deadly shower of metal fragments that could kill and maim hundreds of men caught within range.

French foot soldiers (infantry) from the 1850s demonstrate the different positions used with rifle and bayonet: marching (A), walking long distances (B), defending against foot soldiers (C), attacking infantry (D), and defending against mounted soldiers (E).

SAMUEL COLT

Despite many advances in firing mechanisms, muzzle-loaded firearms were still limited by the time and effort required to load them. One man transformed the design of firearms in the early 19th century—a 21 year-old Connecticut inventor named Samuel Colt (1814–62). In 1836, he patented the design for the first revolver pistol, the Colt Paterson.

The idea was simple, five or six bullets were loaded into a revolving cylinder that was turned by a mechanism linked to the trigger and firing hammer. When one round was fired, the mechanism turned the cylinder and moved a fresh bullet into position ready to be fired. This offered the firer the opportunity to make rapid bursts of shooting without having to reload, and Colt's revolver can be considered the world's first automatic weapon.

At first the new design was not a success, and Colt's factory in Hartford, Connecticut, was only in production for six years before it closed due to lack of business, particularly orders from the U.S. government. His products at first failed to gain many customers thanks to the continued popularity of flintlock and percussion muskets. Colt had to seek other ventures, until his revolvers achieved fame during wars between U.S. troops and Native American fighters in Texas in 1845. When the United States went to war against Mexico the following year, the U.S. Army ordered thousands of revolvers, and Colt had to reopen his factory to cope.

On the heels of this new business, Colt opened new factories in England and in Connecticut. Not only were his designs innovative from a technical point of view, but he also revolutionized the

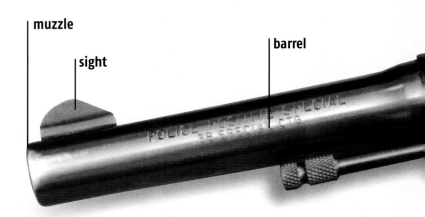

muzzle

sight

barrel

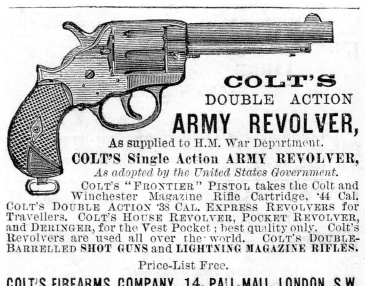

COLT'S DOUBLE ACTION ARMY REVOLVER,
As supplied to H.M. War Department.
COLT'S Single Action ARMY REVOLVER,
As adopted by the United States Government.
COLT'S "FRONTIER" PISTOL takes the Colt and Winchester Magazine Rifle Cartridge, '44 Cal. COLT'S DOUBLE ACTION '38 CAL. EXPRESS REVOLVERS for Travellers. COLT'S HOUSE REVOLVER, POCKET REVOLVER, and DERINGER, for the Vest Pocket; best quality only. Colt's Revolvers are used all over the world. COLT'S DOUBLE-BARRELLED SHOT GUNS and LIGHTNING MAGAZINE RIFLES.

Price-List Free.

COLT'S FIREARMS COMPANY, 14, PALL-MALL, LONDON, S.W.

Agents for Ireland—JOHN RIGBY & Co., Gunmakers, Dublin.

production process by making as much as 80 percent of the components in his products interchangeable. Every part was manufactured by machine tools, not crafted by hand. By 1856, Colt's factories were turning out 150 firearms a day, and he was one of the ten wealthiest businessmen in the United States. Salesmen from the company were welcomed all over the world and Colt's products were bought by customers on every continent. They included almost every major army, as well as private buyers. When Colt died in 1862 at the age of 47, his factories had produced 400,000 weapons and he had amassed a fortune of $15 million, the equivalent of $300 million today.

Samuel Colt holding one of his pistols. These quick-firing weapons changed the way people fought forever. The U.S. Army's main rifle, the M16, is manufactured by Colt's company.

The hammer is raised when the trigger is pulled. When it falls back again, the hammer hits the back of the bullet, igniting the charge, and launching the bullet out of the barrel.

trigger guard

Bullets are loaded into chambers inside the revolving cylinder.

A spring inside the stock (handle) pulls the hammer down on to the bullets in the cylinder.

When pulled, the trigger pushes against the cylinder, turning it around. It also pushes the hammer backward.

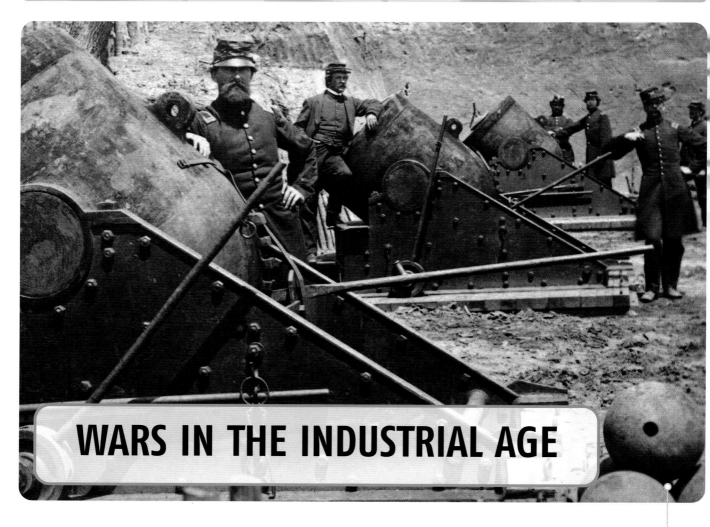

WARS IN THE INDUSTRIAL AGE

Union gunners beside the siege guns used to attack Yorktown, Virginia, in 1862 during the U.S. Civil War. These mortars fired balls more than 1 foot (32 cm) in diameter.

Warfare was transformed during the Industrial Revolution, the process of industrialization that swept through Europe and North America during the last half of the 19th century. Technological advances created rapid-firing small arms, high explosives, and long-range artillery, as well as barbed wire, railroads, motor vehicles, poison gas, aircraft, and telephone and radio communications, all of which had battlefield applications.

Industrialization also created the processes that enabled these weapons to be mass-produced so armies many millions strong could wage wars on a scale never seen before. Warfare became a mass activity, involving many members of a society.

TOTAL WAR
The first wars of the industrial age occurred in the 1860s and 1870s when the United States was rocked by civil war, and Prussia (part of what is now Germany) fought against the Austrians and French in quick succession.

It was the American Civil War (1861–65) that became the first modern "total war," with two huge armies fighting to destroy each other's political and social systems. More Americans died in that war than in any other since.

The conflict set the southern Confederacy states, with their agricultural economy based on slavery, against the industrialized northern Union states, with their larger urban populations. The development of breech-loading rifles—firearms loaded through the side rather than through the muzzle—increased the amount of firepower troops could deliver. In the face of deadly rifle fire, it became impossible for troops to move around the battlefield in solid formations. Breech-loaded artillery guns could be fired more rapidly and produced a huge amount of carnage. When Confederate infantry charged the enemy during the Battle of Gettysburg in 1863, 4,000 soldiers were killed in minutes.

The only way to survive in the face of this furious firepower was to retreat underground into trenches and bunkers. Barbed wire, originally invented to fence cattle, was used to protect defenses and slow down assaults by foot soldiers. The days of the cavalry charge were coming to an end. Horses were now reduced to pulling weapons and supplies to the battlefield.

Key inventions

Machine Guns

Sir Hiram Maxim (1840–1916), an American-born British engineer built the first fully automatic gun, the Maxim gun, in 1883. Ammunition was fed into the weapon by high-pressure gas. Earlier rapid-fire guns, such as the Gatling gun (above) were operated by turning a crank. Heavier guns that fired larger rounds had ammunition fed into them on a cloth or metal belt. Smaller hand-held automatic weapons had bullets in a magazine. By World War I (1914–18) a single machine gunner could kill hundreds of troops approaching across exposed areas of no-man's land.

COLONIAL WARS
European armies spent the last half of the 19th century taking over regions of Africa and Asia, fighting opponents who had far inferior weapons. Soldiers killed hundreds of local fighters with quick-firing rifles, artillery, and even deadlier machine guns.

When facing opponents armed with just spears and swords, the European soldiers formed long lines and fired repeated volleys into the enemy. Small forces could defeat much larger enemy armies by shooting them before they got close enough to use their weapons.

These colonial wars did not drive forward military technology. Although (continued on page 30)

ALFRED NOBEL

Swedish chemist Alfred Nobel (1833–96) had a major influence on the development of weaponry through his work in developing high explosives, including dynamite. Nobel was born into a family of military engineers. His father had been a major supplier of military hardware to Russia during the mid-19th century. Alfred followed in his father's footsteps and studied the chemical properties of explosives in Germany, Italy,

France, and the United States. The most powerful explosive of the time, nitroglycerin, was a highly unstable liquid that was liable to explode if subjected to heat or pressure. It was also very expensive to produce, putting it out of reach for most people who needed it—engineers, miners, and military men.

By 1864, Nobel had solved many of nitroglycerin's stability problems, which meant he could begin to mass-produce dynamite for

Dynamite was generally formed into cylinders, or sticks, as in this haul of explosives discovered by policemen in Los Angeles, California, in 1926. Sticks of dynamite were used to blast away rock for construction purposes. Dynamite was also used in land mines and grenades.

Alfred Nobel regretted the suffering his inventions caused. He left his $9 million fortune to promote peace and understanding.

Civil rights leader Martin Luther King, Jr. receives the Nobel Peace Prize in Oslo, Norway, in 1964.

the first time. He then moved on to trying to make it safer to handle and started mixing the nitroglycerine liquid with sand to create a moldable paste that could be rolled into solid rods. He named this explosive *dynamite*, patenting it in 1867. Nobel then invented detonators, or blasting caps, that allowed dynamite to be ignited using slow-burning fuses. These inventions were welcomed by engineers digging tunnels and cuttings for the railroads that were moving across Europe, Asia, and North America at the time. Nobel was soon a very rich man.

Nobel turned his attention to military technology, and in 1887, his French laboratory invented *ballististe*—a smokeless gunpowder. This totally revolutionized the

design of small arms and made traditional black powder obsolete. It allowed soldiers to fire their weapons without giving away their position with a puff of smoke.

Nobel opened his largest factory at Krummel in Germany to mass produce his new explosive products, and until the end of World War I (1914–18) it employed more than 2,700 workers. There he perfected a version of dynamite dubbed blasting gelatin, which could be molded into different shapes. This was the world's first plastic explosive.

Nobel was not only a skilled chemist and scientist. He was also a clever businessman and set about building a global business empire to market his products. He opened more than 90 factories in Sweden, Germany, France, Scotland, and Italy. His business empire was the first multinational defense company, and many of his inventions were used well into the 20th century.

In spite of growing rich as an arms manufacturer, Nobel was a great sponsor of good causes and supported many peace organizations. On his death, he left his fortune to a foundation to be used to award the prizes for physics, chemistry, medicine, literature, and peace that still bear his name.

Bolt-Action Rifle

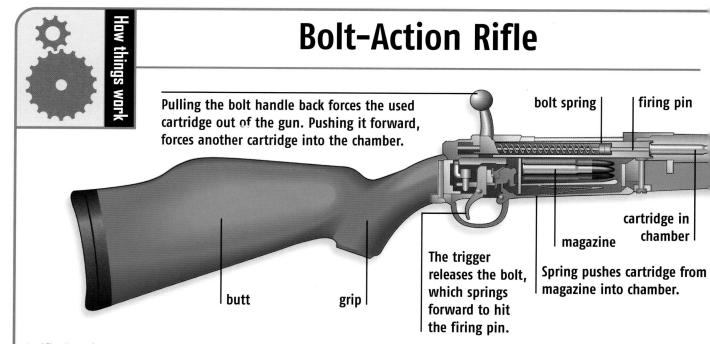

How things work

Pulling the bolt handle back forces the used cartridge out of the gun. Pushing it forward, forces another cartridge into the chamber.

bolt spring

firing pin

butt

grip

The trigger releases the bolt, which springs forward to hit the firing pin.

magazine

cartridge in chamber

Spring pushes cartridge from magazine into chamber.

A rifle is a firearm with a spiral groove cut along the inside of the barrel. This groove makes the bullet spin as it is forced out of the gun. The bullet's spin keeps it flying straight. Bullets fired from a smooth-bore (without rifling) tumble over themselves as they fly and do not follow a straight course. The first rifles were developed in the 16th century in an attempt to make a more accurate weapon for hunting purposes. The first successful hunting rifles were developed in Germany and brought to North America in the late 17th century. By World War I, rifles held ten rounds in a magazine and could hit targets 2,000 feet (600 meters) away.

local people regularly resisted being colonized, they were generally unable to compete with European forces armed with rapid-firing machine guns. European armies learned a hard lesson when they faced more equally matched enemies, such as the Boers of South Africa, whose snipers used rifles to pick off British troops marching into battle.

THE GREAT WAR

World War I (1914–1918) saw modern weapons employed on a mass scale for the first time in Europe. What began as a limited conflict between a handful of European countries spread to engulf most of Europe, the Middle East, and parts of Asia and was fought by troops from as far away as North America and Australia.

It was on the battlefields of France and Belgium that the war was decided, however, and where the greatest amount of killing occurred. In total, 8 million soldiers were killed and 21 million wounded. World War I was also the last major conflict in which military casualties were greater than civilian losses, with some 6 million civilians being killed.

The war was fought between Germany, Austria, and Turkey on one side and France, Britain, and Russia on the other. The British

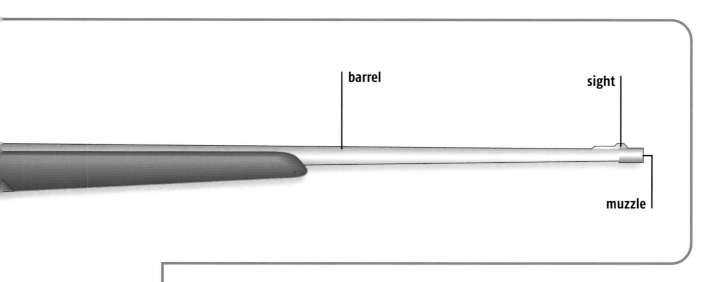

barrel

sight

muzzle

Fact The first rifle to be produced in North America was the Kentucky rifle. This gun was used by American militia during the American Revolution (1775–83).

forces were joined by troops from across the British Empire, including Canada, Australia, Africa, and India. Later in the war, Italy and the United States joined this side, too.

TRENCH WARFARE

The first months of World War I followed the traditional pattern with huge armies maneuvering across Europe, but when they became locked in battle the slaughter was immense. Handguns loaded with magazines—chambers filled with bullets so guns did not need to be repeatedly loaded—

and machine guns, inflicted hundreds of thousands of casualties. This drove the opposing armies to seek shelter in trenches. Trench warfare was a slower but just as brutal affair. Rival armies dug deeper trench lines to protect their troops. Supplies and reinforcements could travel to the front line entirely

Canadian troops go "over the top" of their protective trench while training in France in 1916.

out of sight of the enemy. Tons of concrete were poured to build reinforced bunkers. "No-man's land" between the opposing front lines was filled with barbed wire to delay soldiers advancing across it. Land mines were also laid to hinder any attacks.

The pace of the war soon slowed as each side reinforced their positions. Commanders began looking for ways to break the deadlock. The first solution to be tried was huge artillery barrages. Commanders wanted the guns to blast a path through the enemy barbed wire and shatter their trenches. Field guns could hit targets several miles away, far enough behind the lines to stay safe from enemy infantry. However, the guns had to be targeted by observers who watched the shells fall. Observers

A survivor collects identity papers from an Australian soldier who has been killed in World War I. The battleground in the photograph was once a woodland.

talked to gunners by telephone, connected by miles of wire. Often, however, artillery batteries were forced to fire blind.

ROLLING BARRAGES

The first stage of an infantry assault was for an artillery barrage to roll across the battlefield to force the enemy under cover while troops walked across no-man's land. Crucially, artillery observers could not maintain contact as they moved forward with troops. The barrage had to be moved forward following a strict timetable, regardless of what was happening at the front.

Key inventions

Land Mines

Mines have been used in war for 200 years. The word *mine* came into use because tunnels were dug under enemy positions and packed with gunpowder. This tactic was used in the American Civil War and was another way World War I commanders tried to break the deadlock of trench warfare. Many attacks began with mines exploding (above, 1917) at strongholds along the enemy trench networks. In one mine attack almost a million pounds (450 metric tons) of explosive was placed in a tunnel dug by ex-coal miners under well-defended German positions on Messines Ridge, France, in 1917. The explosion destroyed them completely.

Following World War I, different land mines were developed. Land mines today are metal or plastic containers packed with explosive. They are buried just under the surface of the ground. Most explode when they detect the presence of a person or vehicle above. Others, such as claymore mines, are exploded by defenders as attackers advance over their position. Since 1997, 130 countries have banned the use of land mines because they cause death and injury to civilians even after a conflict has finished. They are still manufactured by companies, however, including American ones.

Flame Throwers

The deepest bunkers were generally immune to artillery fire, and several armies looked at ways to destroy bunkers. Flame throwers were introduced by the Germans in World War I as an antibunker weapon. A jet of gasoline mixed with oil was set on fire, a little like a blowtorch, and the jet was blasted through doors and smaller openings to set a bunker alight. They proved terrifying for defenders, but the users needed to be very brave because the device's fuel tanks had a tendency to explode. In World War II (1939–45) flame throwers were fueled with napalm (above) a flammable gel that stuck to whatever it hit and was very difficult to extinguish.

During the early years of World War I, rolling barrages proved flawed because many bunkers and trenches could survive even the heaviest bombardment. Without observers, there was no way to aim the artillery at pockets of resistance. Without this, enemy machine gunners could emerge from their bunkers and cut down advancing infantry, holding up assaults for days at a time. On the first day of the Somme offensive in July 1916, for example, the British attackers suffered 60,000 casualties, including 19,000 dead, after a seven-day artillery barrage had failed to clear a path through the German defenses.

SPEED AND POWER

Next the British used tracked armored vehicles or tanks to protect their troops as they moved across open ground. Unreliable engines and basic weapons made early tanks slow and ineffective. When the first tanks appeared in 1916, they spread panic among German forces. They soon learned to fight back, however, using the first armor-piercing shells.

It was the Germans who moved next to break the deadlock of trench warfare by forming elite units of stormtroopers to launch surprise attacks against enemy lines. Stormtrooper tactics were revolutionary because they did not

German stormtroopers hide in a shell hole before launching an attack in 1917. They are unloading grenades from a specially trained carrier dog.

of these attacks could disrupt large areas of the front, opening the way for more heavily armed troops to move forward.

Exhaustion and war weariness began to spread through both sides as World War I dragged on into its fourth year. Russia withdrew from the war when it was rocked by revolution. By November 1918, Germany sued for peace as American, British, and French soldiers staged a huge fall offensive.

rely on huge artillery support and large attack formations. Small groups of soldiers worked at night close up to the enemy. They had small field guns, hand grenades, and flame throwers to knock out enemy bunkers without the need for artillery. Rather than wait for back up troops to help them, the stormtroopers carried on fighting deep into the enemy territory, causing chaos. Several

World War I was a battle of endurance and had an incredible cost in human life. The armed forces looked for ways to break the deadlock of trench warfare. The German Army opted to combine tanks and aircraft with the stormtrooper tactics. Their *Blitzkrieg* ("lightning-war") tactics, used to conquer Europe in 1939 and 1940, was the result.

Tank F.4

World War I tanks, such as this British model, were designed to cross the shell-holed ground between trenches.

1. Crew used movable guns to attack enemy defenses.

2. The whole tank was covered in thick, steel armor. This made it very heavy, and the tank's engine could only produce slow speeds.

3. Caterpillar tracks were much better at covering rough ground than wheeled vehicles.

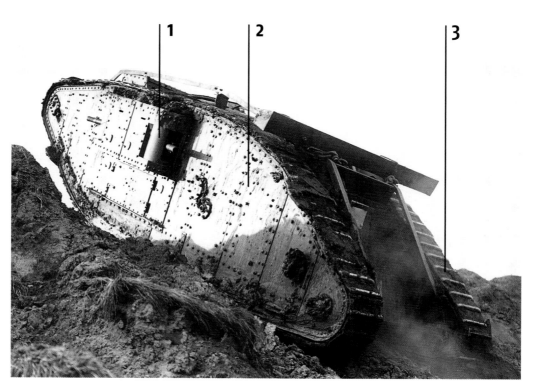

1   2   3

GAS, GAS, GAS!

As World War I slowed to a bloody stalemate at the end of 1914, German commanders began to look at radical ways to get troops through the enemy's front line. The British navy was preventing any supply ships from reaching German ports, and the country was rapidly running out of nitrates, a chemical used in explosives.

German chemist Dr. Fritz Haber proposed engulfing British and French trenches with clouds of poisonous gas to create panic and allow German troops to take them over. He suggested using

chlorine, a choking and corrosive gas. However, it took several months before he could work out an effective way of using this new, terrifying weapon.

By March 1915, thousands of cylinders of chlorine were in place around the town of Ypres, Belgium. The Germans waited for several days until the wind was blowing toward the French lines, and then they released the gas. The effect was dramatic as the cloud enveloped unprotected French troops. In a matter of minutes 5,000 soldiers were dead and 10,000 unable to

British soldiers injured by mustard gas in World War I, line up as they prepare to leave the front line. Many of them have been blinded by the blistering effects of the chemical weapon.

It was not just people that needed protecting from poisonous gas. These German transport horses are equipped with gas masks, just as are their riders.

fight. Thousands more fled in panic. The result was far more successful than the Germans expected, and they did not have enough troops ready to occupy all the land available.

Over the next three years gas warfare became more commonplace as new chemical agents were developed. The most deadly one was called mustard gas because of its distinctive smell. This was a blister agent that caused terrible burns on contact with the skin or the inside of victims' lungs. Artillery shells were designed to carry the gas to the enemy, so there was no need to wait for favorable winds. Mortars fired the shells in a high curve, dropping them directly into enemy trenches so their occupants had little time to put on protective equipment.

Following a gas attack, attacking troops had to move into the affected area quickly but carefully. The wind dispersed gas weapons in just a few minutes. However, sheltered areas like bunkers held the deadly gases for several hours after an attack.

Protective clothing and masks were used to defend against gas. The first gas masks were cloths soaked in soldiers' urine. Later models contained more sophisticated filters, and capes covered the skin to protect against blister agents. Early warnings of an impending gas attack were also vital for troops to put on their protective equipment. Canaries and other caged animals were used as early warning devices. Canaries are generally affected by the gas more quickly than people, so troops had time to protect themselves. As protective equipment and clothing became more widespread the effectiveness of gas attacks were reduced. Troops became more confident and did not panic when they came under gas attack, reducing casualties and the advantages of using chemical weapons. By the end of World War I, both sides had used large amounts of poisonous gas weapons.

INNOVATIONS OF WWII

Between 1939 and 1945 the world was engulfed by World War II (WWII), the most widespread conflict the world has ever seen. This was a war between Germany, Italy, and Japan on one side versus, the United States, Russia, Britain, and several other allies. These nations had to harness all of their resources to ensure their survival. Millions of civilians were killed in their homes or systematically exterminated in death camps, while fighters died in battles across the globe, on land, in the air, and both on and beneath the ocean.

While determination, firepower, and luck were always crucial for winning battles, new technology played a role in several decisive victories for both sides. Enormous investments were made in military research and new weapons were frequently developed as the world's most gifted minds turned their attention to war work.

EYE IN THE SKY

World War II was the first conflict in which air power was essential for winning battles. New designs of aircraft appeared regularly, equipped with more powerful engines and able to carry more, superior armaments.

Just as importantly, new systems were developed to detect and defend against attacking aircraft. Radar allowed enemy aircraft to be detected at hundreds of miles away by bouncing a radio signal off them. This proved its worth in the Battle of Britain in 1940.

A Russian T-34 tank, the most advanced armored vehicle of its age. When it entered service in the 1940s, it was the first tank to have wide tracks and thick, sloping armor.

Radar alerted the Royal Air Force to approaching German bombers, allowing fighters to intercept them before they reached their targets. Radar sets were also mounted in warplanes to allow them to seek out enemy bombers flying at night. The importance of radar was soon recognized by both sides and great efforts were put into defeating it. Transmitters were used to interfere with radar signals, and plane loads of metal foil strips were dropped to create false radar signals.

AIR OPERATIONS

The biplanes of World War I were soon replaced by single-winged machines. Fighter aircraft such as the Spitfire, Messerschmitt Me-109, and P-51 Mustang were the fastest and most maneuverable airplanes of their day. As well as attacking troops on the ground during battles, fighter aircraft were used to defend against enemy bombers that were heading for cities and industrial centers. Each side was trying to smash the morale of the civilian population with relentless bombing raids, and began to develop fleets of mightier bomber aircraft. By 1942 four-engine heavy bombers, such as the British Lancaster and U.S. B-17 Flying Fortress, were pounding German and Japanese cities day and night.

As well as bombers, each side developed large transport aircraft. These were used in the first airborne operations. The first German troops into Norway, for example, arrived by parachute or landed in gliders in 1940.

No longer able to compete with British and U.S. air power, the German forces began to use rockets and missiles to hit at civilian targets. From the fall of 1944, the Germans bombarded London in the first long-distance

A German radar transmitter used to detect approaching aircraft. The transmitter produced radio waves, which reflected off metal aircraft. These reflections were picked up by the radar system so operators could see the planes even when they were many miles away.

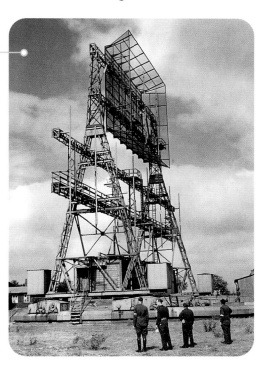

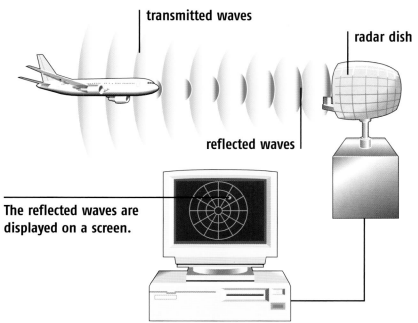

transmitted waves

radar dish

reflected waves

The reflected waves are displayed on a screen.

missile campaign. Over eight months, 2,500 V-2 rockets were fired at London, the British capital, and Antwerp, Belgium, with 3,000 people killed and 7,000 wounded in London alone.

MECHANIZED ARMIES

The land battles of WWII were fought by highly mobile units of armored vehicles, such as tanks. These weapons played a crucial role in the German *Blitzkrieg* (lightning-war) tactics, which they used to take over most of Europe. Blitzkrieg involved attacking the enemy with aircraft and artillery over a wide area, while columns of tanks and infantry moved forward rapidly into enemy territory.

These tactics were almost unstoppable until a revolutionary Russian tank was designed. The T-34 was the first tank to have sloping armor, which made it more likely that enemy shells would bounce off rather than damage the vehicle. Compared to previous tanks, T-34s also had very wide tracks—similar to the widths of modern tank tracks—which gripped the ground and made the tanks highly maneuverable, even on the most treacherous terrain.

The Germans countered the threat of the T-34 by producing the monster Tiger tank, which had armor 4 inches (10 cm) thick and *Panzers* (Panthers), which had sloped armor like the T-34. In 1943, 2,700 Panzers and Tiger tanks supported by nearly half a million German troops met 1.5 million Soviet soldiers armed with nearly 5,000 tanks and armored vehicles at Kursk, Ukraine. The resulting fight was the greatest tank battle of all time and proved to be the turning point of WWII, with the Russians forcing the Germans into a long retreat.

LAND AND SEA

On many occasions the United States and Britain had to move large assault forces from ships out

Key inventions

Faster Warplanes

Germany's scientists were at the forefront of developing rockets and jet-powered aircraft. The rocket-powered Messerschmitt Me-163 Komet was the fastest aircraft of the war being able to fly faster than 600 mph (960 km/h), but it was very hard to fly and few pilots survived to tell the tale of their missions. The Me-262 fighter (above) had two jet engines. It was a more practical weapon, giving enemy pilots a major scare when it entered service in 1944. Production problems meant the Germans built less than a thousand. The German jet did prompt the British air force into rushing their own jet fighter, the Gloster Meteor, into service before the end of the war.

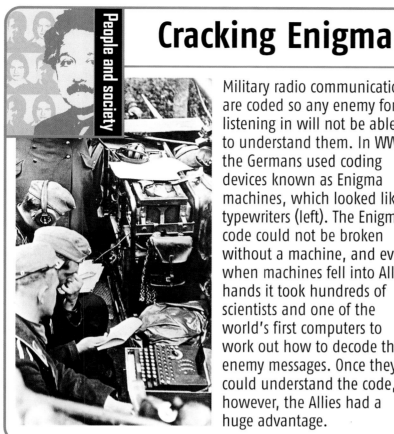

People and society

Cracking Enigma

Military radio communications are coded so any enemy force listening in will not be able to understand them. In WWII, the Germans used coding devices known as Enigma machines, which looked like typewriters (left). The Enigma's code could not be broken without a machine, and even when machines fell into Allied hands it took hundreds of scientists and one of the world's first computers to work out how to decode the enemy messages. Once they could understand the code, however, the Allies had a huge advantage.

Trucks called DUKWs—or "ducks"—were fitted with both wheels and propellers and enclosed in boat-shaped hulls so supplies and troops could be literally driven up beaches or across rivers. Large landing craft and ships were built that could sail into shallow water or even beach on dry land so troops could storm ashore.

RADIO CONTROLLED

World War II was the first large conflict to use radio as the main means of communication. Radios were reliable enough to be used by all arms of the military. They were installed into aircraft, in tanks, and on ships, and sturdy field radios were carried by soldiers so commanders could talk to their units while in the midst of the fighting.

A U.S. Army DUKW, or "duck" drives on to land. The driver could either connect the engine to the wheels or to a boat propeller.

at sea onto land. They developed a broad range of equipment to put armies ashore on enemy-held coastlines. Amphibious attacks were used to invade France, Italy, North Africa, and many Japanese-held Pacific islands. Tanks were fitted with screens and propellers to allow them to float ashore.

This communications revolution enabled operations to take place much more quickly. Artillery spotters, for example, did not have to be connected to gunners by telephone cables. They could move around the battlefield with the troops and target barrages accurately. Ground commanders could also coordinate warplanes in the skies above the fighting for the first time.

In the space of six years of unrelenting warfare, military technology advanced at a tremendous pace. Much of it had uses in peacetime, opening the way for a fast passenger aircraft, radio communications, computers, and space travel.

boat-shaped hull

MISSILE ATTACK

During World War II, the German military developed the world's first powered missiles that were designed to carry bombs over long distances without the need for a crew. One of the missiles was the V-1. V-1s were jet-powered pilotless aircraft. They were used as the first guided missiles. The V-1's more powerful cousin, the V-2 was a rocket that flew at four times the speed of sound.

The V-2 program was started by the German army early in the war, but the air force began to develop V-1s when the V-2 project began

to hit problems. The first V-1 prototype flew at the end of 1941, launching from a ramp.

Unlike cruise missiles today, V-1s could not change course once in the air. They were aimed at the target, and their engines were timed to run just long enough to reach their destination. The V-1 was 25 feet (7.6 m) long and flew at 360 mph (580 km/h). They had a range of 155 miles (250 km), when they then fell from the sky, carrying a ton of explosive onto a target.

The first V-1s were used in action on June 12, 1941, to bombard London. Over the

A V-1 missile is prepared for launch. The bomb was powered by a pulse jet, the large tube at the top. This engine produced bursts of thrust, rather than a constant stream like modern jet engines.

A V-1 "doodlebug" falls toward houses in a town in southern England. These flying bombs did not cause as much damage as bomber raids, but they terrified the people on the ground.

next 10 months more than 18,000 were fired at targets in England, France, and Belgium. The start of this V-1 campaign had been delayed by a bombing campaign that destroyed the concrete launch sites in northern France. In response to this, the Germans built prefabricated launch ramps that could be erected in a few hours and were difficult for Allied spotter planes to find.

Some 10,000 V-1s were fired at London alone, killing 6,000 and injuring 40,000, as well as destroying 20,000 homes. The V-1s were soon nicknamed "doodlebugs" and "buzz bombs" by the British because of their distinctive sound. War weary Londoners quickly learned to take cover when they heard a V-1's jet engine cut out, indicating it was about to fall to earth. Antiaircraft batteries and fighter planes guarded the routes taken by the missiles. Due to the fact that V-1s flew straight and level at a constant altitude, they were relatively easy to shoot down. Fighter aircraft also tried to nudge the V-1s off course by tipping their wings. This effort resulted in almost one half of all V-1s being destroyed or diverted away from populated areas. The Germans fought back by developing an air-launched version, so V-1s could be fired from unexpected directions.

The V-1 was the first guided missile to be successfully used in combat and was the precursor of many modern weapons systems. Both the Americans and Russians seized many discarded V-1s and V-2s from the ruins of the defeated Nazi Germany. The missile and rocket technology was used to create ballistic missiles and accurate guided missiles, such as the U.S. Tomahawk.

THE MANHATTAN PROJECT

A mushroom cloud rises 60,000 feet (18,000 m) above Nagasaki, Japan in 1945. The cloud was caused by a U.S. atomic bomb.

This team of scientists from the University of Chicago led by Enrico Fermi (center) were the first to create a fission reaction in 1942. This made nuclear weapons possible.

The Manhattan Project was the secret code name for the efforts of the United States to develop nuclear bombs during World War II. The project had been launched early in 1942 after a committee of leading American and British nuclear physicists had told U.S. President Franklin D. Roosevelt that it was possible to harness the power released by atomic fission (splitting atoms) to cause a powerful explosion.

RACE AGAINST TIME

Intelligence reports suggested that Germany's Nazi regime was also looking at developing an atomic weapon. This led the United States to put unlimited resources into building the weapon to ensure they and their allies had it first. It was recognized, even at this early stage, that the atomic bomb would transform warfare and give whoever possessed it a huge advantage. The Nazis could not be allowed to get the atomic bomb first. The projected budget for the bomb was enormous by 1942 standards—more than $100 million—and those involved were told they could have everything they needed to ensure success.

Initial efforts revolved around securing supplies of the key ingredients for nuclear weapons: uranium and plutonium. These radioactive metals are known as fissionable materials because they decay (break down) into other substances while releasing huge amounts of heat, light, and more deadly forms of radiation. Plutonium decays much faster than uranium and there is none left on Earth, so it had to be made inside a reactor from uranium. The uranium used in bombs was purified, or enriched, so it contained more of the most radioactive type of atom. Five methods were considered to enrich uranium, and they were all attempted to make sure enough uranium was produced.

NUCLEAR LAB

While plutonium was being made at the Hanford Site in central Washington, an elite team of

"Little Boy" Uranium Bomb

A radar unit measures the altitude of the bomb as it falls. The bomb explodes at a set height above the ground.

Larger "target" of uranium is hit by wedge, reaches critical mass and explodes.

uranium wedge

barrel

A nonnuclear explosive fires wedge of uranium down barrel.

"Fat Boy" Plutonium Bomb

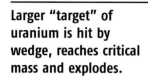

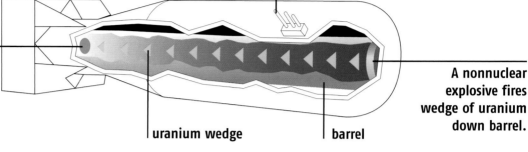

plutonium core

Nonnuclear explosive squeezes sphere and core together, causing nuclear explosion.

plutonium sphere

nuclear scientists began working on the design of the bomb itself at an isolated laboratory at Los Alamos in the hills of New Mexico.

The scientists were concerned that they might cause a premature explosion while they figured out how to build a bomb. They knew fissionable material would explode if it was collected together into a large enough lump, or a "critical mass." It was decided to bring two small pieces together so they formed a critical mass and exploded. Two methods of forcing the fissionable material together were considered. For uranium bombs, they designed a gun

detonation system, which involved a quantity of uranium being fired down a gun barrel at another piece. Plutonium is a more stable material and a spherical detonation device was designed. This involved a plutonium core ringed with a plutonium casing. The two pieces of metal were forced together at high speed using a powerful high explosive.

TEST SITE

Delays in producing the required quantities of fissionable material prevented the first bombs from being ready until the summer of 1945. Germany was by then out of

The ground crew of Enola Gay, the B-29 that dropped the "Little Boy" bomb on Hiroshima, Japan in 1945, pose with Paul Tibbets, the aircraft's pilot (center, with pipe).

the war, and the U.S. president, Harry S. Truman (1884–1972), decided to use the new weapons to deliver a knock-out blow against Japan. He hoped Japan would surrender afterward, so U.S. forces would not have to invade Japan, resulting in the deaths of many more millions of people.

Enriched uranium was in short supply, but the project scientists were confident that their uranium bomb, dubbed "Little Boy," would work. It was decided not to test it before the weapon was used in

warfare. The plutonium bomb, nicknamed "Fat Boy," was tested in the New Mexico desert at the Trinity Test Site on July 16, 1945. The world's first ever atomic explosion proved the weapon was immensely more powerful than had been imagined. The tower securing the weapon vaporized, windows 200 miles (320 km) away were blown out, a 25-foot (7.6-m) crater was gouged in the earth, and desert sand around the blast point, or "ground zero," was melted into glass.

NUCLEAR ATTACK

President Truman ordered the atomic weapons to be moved to bases in the Pacific ready to be used against Japan at the earliest opportunity. A special unit of the U.S. Army Air Corps equipped with the Boeing B-29 Superfortresses, the biggest bomber in America's arsenal, was formed to deliver the weapons. By early August they were based on the Pacific island of Tinian and ready to begin the world's first and only atomic attacks. Only when the pilots and crews of the squadron were on Tinian were they told about the secret of their deadly mission. The port city of Hiroshima in southwestern Japan was selected as the first target for a "Little Boy" bomb. The city had been largely untouched by earlier U.S. air raids and so the power of the weapon could properly be assessed.

At 9:15 am on August 6, a B-29, nicknamed "Enola Gay" after the pilot's wife, dropped the bomb over Hiroshima. It was a clear day and the crew of the aircraft had a grandstand view of the weapon's devastating effect. The blinding flash of the immense fireball lit up the sky before the explosion started to rise into the distinctive mushroom cloud. Then the aircraft was rocked by a violent shock wave as it turned for home.

The ruins of Hiroshima a few days after it became the first city to be attacked with an atomic bomb. The domed building in the background is still standing today.

Hiroshima's Peace Park today contains the ruins of the Industrial Promotion Hall now named the Atomic Bomb Dome. This building is the closest ruin to ground zero.

On the ground, people and most buildings near ground zero were vaporized. Those in the open were scorched by the heat of the flash and suffered terrible burns. The heat set large parts of the city on fire, and the fires were fanned by high winds caused by shock waves. Debris and rubble were sucked up into the sky by the rising fire ball and were mixed with the radioactive remains of the bomb's uranium. This fell to earth, polluting the city and causing radiation sickness among thousands more people, who died lingering deaths over the next few weeks. About 78,000 people were killed outright and more than 80,000 were injured. Another 20,000 died later as a result of the bombing, and the remains of 4,000 people were never found.

The Japanese government was stunned by the weapon but decided to fight on. Three days later, on August 9, a plutonium bomb was dropped on the Japanese city of Nagasaki. The weapon proved not as powerful as the Hiroshima bomb, and the city's geography shielded much of its population, so casualties were less—40,000 killed and 25,000 wounded. Within days of the second bomb attack, the Japanese surrendered, and the world entered the nuclear age.

MUTUAL ASSURED DESTRUCTION

The end of World War II in 1945 heralded another confrontation between the capitalist West led by the United States and the communist Eastern Bloc under the leadership of the Soviet Union. This confrontation never developed into a full-scale "hot" war, but a nuclear standoff that continued until the 1990s became known as the Cold War.

Until 1949, only the United States had nuclear weapons. In that year the Soviet Union tested its own bomb, triggering an arms race as each side tried to become more powerful than the other.

DETERRENCE
Although at times both sides considered launching nuclear attacks, military strategists soon came to the conclusion that a nuclear war would be disastrous for everyone.

The only way to deter the other side from launching a surprise attack was to ensure that a large force of nuclear weapons would always survive the attack and be ready to launch a devastating counterattack. This was the logic of *Mutual Assured Destruction,* or MAD, that became central to the Cold War nuclear strategies.

A U.S. Trident missile is test-fired from a submerged submarine. Missiles like this are carried by nuclear-powered submarines. They can hit anywhere on Earth with nuclear warheads.

At first nuclear arsenals were maintained independently, but the U.S. and Soviet Union entered into a series of arms-control treaties that ensured they were always both equally capable of destroying each other. Both sides also agreed not to build defensive weapons systems that could destroy waves of enemy nuclear bombs or missiles before they could hit their intended target. The U.S. and Soviet populations needed to be vulnerable to nuclear annihilation. That was the main guarantee that neither side would be foolish enough to risk attempting a nuclear first strike.

Key inventions

Eye in the Sky

The first Soviet atom bomb test in 1949 made U.S. leaders determined to find out the true scale of the military threat posed by the Soviets. They built a spyplane that could overfly the enemy at the edge of space to photograph key facilities. The result was the famous U-2 that overflew the Soviet Union many times until one was shot down in 1960. Spyplanes were also used during the Cuban missile crisis of 1962 to monitor Soviet missiles being taken to the Caribbean (above). Their surveillance role was taken over by space-based spy satellites, launched by NASA during the early days of space exploration.

BOMBER FLEETS

The MAD strategy drove a relentless pace of technological development to prevent either the U.S. or Soviet nuclear force being destroyed in a surprise attack. The first U.S. atomic bombs were carried by a fleet of Boeing B-29 Stratofortress strategic bombers. Through into the 1950s, these aircraft were the main delivery system for America's nuclear arsenal. Even though the propeller-powered B-29s could fly high and boasted a formidable defensive firepower, by the early 1950s, they had become very vulnerable to the Soviet's new jet-powered MiG-15 fighters.

The United States Air Force turned to the American aircraft industry to build it a long-range jet-powered bomber aircraft that could carry weapons into Soviet territory if needed. Boeing B-47 Stratojets, powered by six jet engines began carrying the U.S. atom bombs, but these were soon replaced by the eight-engined B-52 Stratofortress. As well as these Boeing aircraft, the Convair company developed the delta-winged B-58 Hustler. This high-speed jet was designed to carry weapons on low-level missions.

Strategic Air Command's (SAC) bombers needed to spend long periods patroling over the North Pole, ready to strike at targets deep inside the Soviet Union. A fleet of jet-powered KC-135 tankers aircraft were used to refuel the bombers in mid-air.

EARLY WARNING

The Soviet Union responded by developing its own fleet of heavy bombers to strike at the United States and its allies. To provide warning of attack, both sides built long chains of radar stations along their borders. The U.S. stations ran from Alaska through Greenland to Britain. At its air bases, SAC kept a large part of the U.S. bomber fleet on alert, ready to take off at a few minutes notice. Armed bombers were kept in the air for many hours at a time, to keep them safe from surprise attack on the ground.

To counteract the power of SAC's bombers, the Soviet Union began developing long-range missiles. When it launched its *Sputnik* space satellite in 1957, the Soviet Union revealed an ability to deliver nuclear weapons by missiles that could be fired into space before falling back to Earth. These new weapons could arrive at targets anywhere on Earth minutes after launch. With so little warning, missiles made bomber forces, which had so far kept the peace during the Cold War, completely obsolete.

SILENT FORCE

Huge missile forces were rushed into production by both sides, but these sensitive devices were unreliable and very vulnerable to a surprise first strike. They were protected in deep concrete silos until they were ready to fire.

Instead of storing missiles in bunkers, the Soviet military kept their missiles safe from attack by keeping them constantly on the move. Missiles were always ready to go on mobile launchers.

Early Warning System

People and society

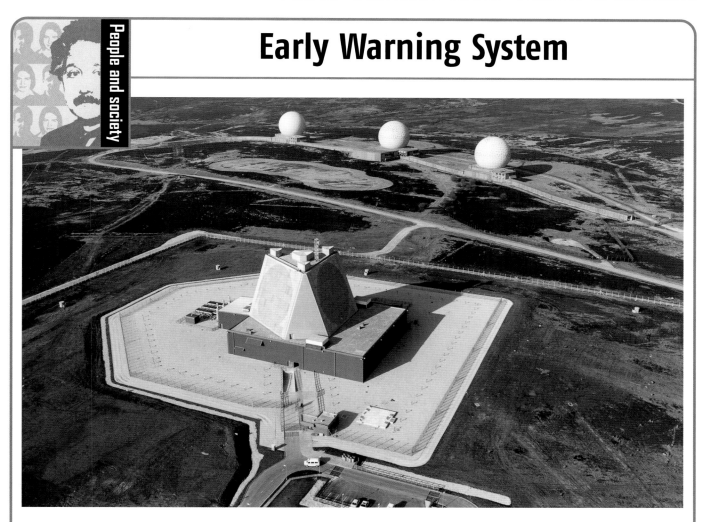

From the 1950s, North American Air Defense Command (NORAD) was crucial to the U.S. defense plan. Buried deep under Cheyenne Mountain outside Colorado Springs, Colorado, NORAD controlled a network of radar stations (above, in Yorkshire, England) and interceptor fighters. Its job was to give nuclear-armed bombers time to become airborne if the United States was attacked, and allow the U.S. president to make the key decision on what sort of retaliation to order.

As well as land-based missiles, nuclear weapons were also carried by submarines. Huge nuclear-powered submarines could remain hidden deep underwater, keeping their missiles safe from detection and attack. Ballistic-missile firing submarines, such as the U.S. Polaris and Soviet Typhoon class boats, are the ultimate weapons of nuclear deterrence. Their captains are issued with orders to open fire if they know their country is under nuclear attack, or even if they lose contact with their commanders. With each boat carrying nearly 50 missiles, each fitted with multiple warheads (individual weapons), no matter how successful a land-based missile or bomber strike had been, the resulting retaliation from the invisible submarine force is enough to make even the most militaristic leader think twice about initiating a nuclear war.

ICBM

Intercontinental Ballistic Missiles (ICBMs) were the key weapons of the Cold War. Unlike bombers or submarines, which could also be used in conventional war, the ICBM was designed purely as a weapon of mass destruction. Because they are meant as a deterrence, they have never been used in warfare.

Ballistic missiles are powered into space by rocket motors and then fall back to earth, using gravity to pull them back through the atmosphere. Small thrusters are fired while the missile is in space to position it for reentry so it falls to Earth at the right point. Nuclear weapons are designed to blow up above the target so their explosive power spreads outward, rather than being wasted creating a crater.

The first ballistic missile to be used in battle was the German V-2 fired during World War II. Many of the V-2's designers worked in U.S. or Soviet missile programs during the 1950s.

The first true ICBMs entered service in the early 1960s. They were targeted to fly over the North Pole—the shortest route to the enemy. These early missiles used highly dangerous liquid oxygen to power their rocket engines. This fuel could only be pumped into the weapons immediately before launch. The risk of explosion made it too dangerous to house these missiles underground in silos, and they took up to an hour to fuel, making them very vulnerable to a first strike.

A V-2 rocket is fueled before being fired in 1945. These missiles could fly 210 miles (336 km). They traveled so fast that no one could hear them coming.

A technician examines the warhead of a Minuteman ICBM inside its silo. This missile carries three nuclear warheads.

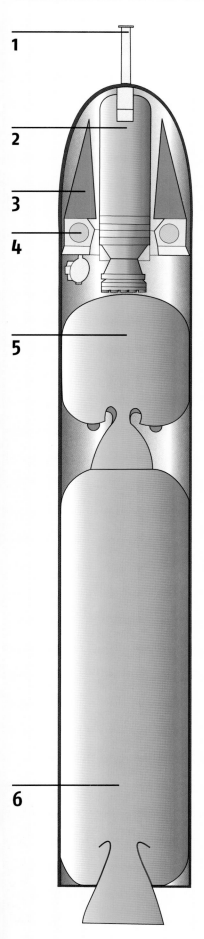

Trident II Missile

Trident II missiles carried on U.S. and British nuclear submarines. They are launched under water and can fly more than 4,100 miles (6,600 km).

1. The aerospike reduces drag as the missile flies through air.

2. The third-stage rocket motor positions the warheads above their target while in space.

3. The missile has five warheads.

4. The equipment section contains the guidance and targeting systems.

5. The second stage rocket motor provides an extra boost to get the missile into space.

6. The first stage motor is used to launch the missile. Like the other stages, this motor is powered by solid rocket fuel.

H-Bomb Warhead

This is one of several designs of a thermonuclear device. The fission device is a small nuclear bomb that explodes creating huge temperatures. This causes the lithium deuteride to release radioactive hydrogen, which fuse with each other releasing yet more energy. This second explosion causes a third in the uranium jacket.

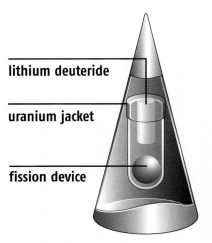

lithium deuteride

uranium jacket

fission device

The development of solid rocket fuel meant ICBMs could be based underground in silos and, more crucially, carried to sea in nuclear-powered submarines.

The next breakthrough was the development of multiple reentry vehicle (MRV) warheads, which allowed a single missile to carry up to 15 individual warheads or decoys. These missiles release their individual warheads while in space, which reenter the atmosphere and travel to different targets. Swamping the enemy's radar network with hundreds of reentry vehicles, both real warheads and decoys, was intended to confuse its defenses and make it more likely that a higher percentage of the warheads would get through to their targets.

Starting in the 1970s, the Soviet Union and United States signed a series of arms-control treaties to limit the number of ICBMs each country could deploy, and the number of MRV warheads they had. This prevented the nuclear arms race from getting out of control and made each side confident that the other side was not trying to gain an advantage. Both sides agreed to park their bombers in the open and for silos to be opened so satellites could count them.

MODERN WARFARE

The Cold War ended in 1991 when the Soviet Union collapsed, and the communist regimes of Eastern Europe were overthrown. Despite hostilities between East and West coming to end, the world continued to be rocked by wars, including the Persian Gulf War in 1991 and many civil wars across the globe.

BATTLE TANKS
Modern military hardware, such as tanks, artillery, and missiles, do not seem to have changed much in outward appearance from those used in the 1960s and 1970s.

However, computer technology has revolutionized weapon design and transformed the way wars are now fought. Today weapons are safer to use, more reliable, and deadlier than ever before.

The tank is still the main weapon system of land warfare, and it boasts features unknown at the height of the Cold War. Vehicles such as the U.S. M1A2 Abrams, British Challenger 2, and French LeClerc tanks are now almost invulnerable to enemy attack thanks to their composite armor. This armor is made of a mixture of steel and ceramic

Two U.S. infantry troops run for cover during a skirmish in Somalia in 1993. As well as being armed with a rifle, the leading soldier is carrying a missile launcher on his back.

M551 Sheridan

This small tank is used by American airborne forces. The tank is small enough to be carried to the battlefield in airplanes.

1. The tank's commander travels in the movable turret and uses the vehicle's machine gun.

2. The driver sits in the front of the tank underneath the gun turret. The other two crew sit behind him.

3. The gun can fire both missiles and shells.

4. The tank's diesel engine is positioned at the back.

5. The tank carries eight antitank missiles

6. Supplies of engine fuel are carried on board.

7. The high-explosive shells have hard metal tips to smash through armor.

plates. Not only is this stronger than armor made of solid metal plate, it is also lighter. This saving in weight makes mighty battle tanks more fuel-efficient and allows them to reach higher speeds. The United States military also protects its tanks with extra plates of depleted uranium—a very dense and hard metal made from spent nuclear fuel.

Modern tanks also fire shells tipped with depleted uranium, or tungsten, another hard metal. These dart-shaped rounds can punch a hole through tanks with the even thickest steel armor. The

radioactive dust left behind by uranium shells is feared to cause health problems when breathed in.

The tank is such a powerful weapons system because not only is it almost immune to attack, but its immense firepower can also be used at any time, day or night and in any weather conditions. Gun sights and other imaging systems used by tank crews can detect the heat produced by enemy tanks more than 1.25 miles (2 km) away. Tank gunners can hit enemy vehicles at night before the enemy even knows the tanks are there. (*Continued on page 60.*)

INFANTRY

The infantry soldier of the 21st century is a highly trained and well equipped fighting machine. He is armed with an automatic rifle capable of firing hundreds of rounds per minute at targets more than 2,000 feet (600 m) away. Most modern armies have reduced the caliber (width) of the bullets fired by infantry rifles by about 30 percent. This reduces the range at which infantry weapons can hit targets easily, but it increases the number of bullets that each soldier can carry. Despite their large firepower, infantrymen are still issued with a bayonet to stab enemy troops during hand-to-hand combat.

Added firepower comes from a grenade launcher that may be fitted underneath the rifle. Infantry soldiers are often equipped with throwaway antitank rockets, which they use to take on tanks or destroy enemy bunkers.

Modern soldiers are all issued with body armor and tough helmets that protect them against shrapnel (shell fragments). Body armor is

A squad of infantry fans out while on patrol. The soldiers are transported in a "humvee" or HMMWV—a high-mobility multipurpose wheeled vehicle.

1

2

made of a very tough fabric called Kevlar. This is tightly woven to prevent high-speed objects from getting through it. The armor is sometimes strengthened with metal or carbon-fiber plates. Metal helmets have been replaced by lightweight glass-fiber head gear, which is strong enough to protect against a high-speed bullet. Soldiers use radios inside their helmets to talk with their comrades. In the future, these radios will also send pictures and maps between individuals.

The modern infantry soldier does not fight alone, but operates as part of a four-

A soldier using a night-vision scope. Infantry often attacks at night, and soldiers using heat-sensitive equipment can see almost as well as during the day.

person fire team. This team works together to provide covering fire as it moves. Teams usually move around the battlefield in an infantry fighting vehicle or helicopter. Two teams are grouped

together into a squad that can work together to defend a position or attack a strongly held enemy position. Four squads make up a platoon.

Infantry forces must be as ready to keep the peace as fight wars. Peacekeeping troops use equipment not normally issued to combat troops, such as satellite radios, engineering gear, and mine-detection devices.

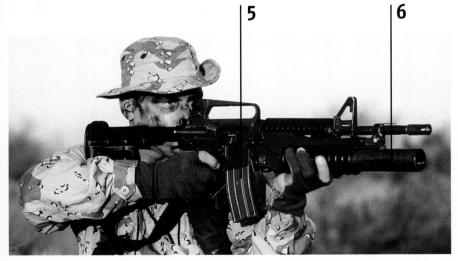

5

6

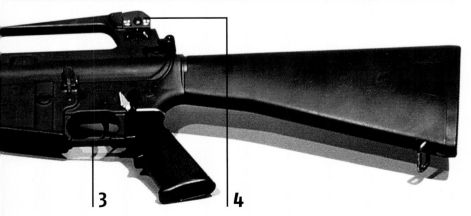

3

4

M16 Rifle

The M16 rifle has been used by U.S. forces since 1967. It is still the main infantry rifle in use today. The rifle can fire up to three rounds in repeated bursts.

1. A supressor on the muzzle reduces the flash produced by each shot.

2. The barrel grip can be fitted with a handle for rapid firing.

3. The trigger guard opens so a soldier wearing mitts can still fire the gun.

4. Rear sight on the handle can be replaced with a more powerful telescopic sight.

5. The magazine contains 30 bullets. High-pressure gas pushes them into the firing chamber.

6. A grenade launcher can be fitted beneath the barrel.

Antitank Missiles

Infantry of the 21st century is armed with lightweight antitank missiles that are guided to their target by remote control. Earlier models, such as the American TOW and Soviet Sagger, used wires trailed behind the missile to transmit guidance instructions. Newer weapons, such as the Hellfire or Javelin (above), are guided by laser beam or radio signals. These slow-flying missiles are able to penetrate tank armor with a jet of superheated molten metal that punches through a tank's skin.

DEEP BATTLE

Weapons are now more accurate and lethal than ever, and battles are being fought over a huge area with opposing forces often ranged many miles apart from each other. By the end of the 20th century, modern military forces were reorganized to fight these so-called "deep battles." The weapons used are designed to hit enemy reserve troops and supply systems many miles behind the enemy front line.

In World War II (1939–45) this sort of job was carried out by fighter-bombers and heavy artillery guns, but there was always a problem of locating and then hitting the correct targets. Modern armies can now see anywhere on the battlefield with spy satellites or uncrewed spotter planes. Once they select a target they have an array of long-range weapons to attack it with. These include launchers that fire missiles, which release hundreds of deadly bomblets over targets spread over a wide area, such as supply dumps, truck parks, and headquarters complexes. More artillery guns can now fire shells up to 25 miles (40 km). These long-range rounds are given an extra push by rocket boosters. They are also guided by laser and can hit the same target repeatedly.

HELICOPTER ATTACK

Perhaps the most potent deep-battle weapon is the attack helicopter, such as the American AH-64 Apache and Russian Mi-24 HINDs. These are designed to fly ahead of tank columns, hitting enemy armored vehicles and heading off enemy counterattacks. The pilots are protected in heavily armored cockpits and have high-powered night-vision devices to help them direct a deadly array of weaponry against targets. These include machine guns to shoot at ground troops or the occupants of unarmored vehicles, unguided rockets to hit targets spread over wide areas, and guided missiles to destroy tanks with great precision.

The first attack helicopters saw service during the Vietnam War (1946–75). They were armed with wire-guided missiles, which required the helicopter to hover or fly straight to hit a target. The latest attack helicopters have "fire-and-forget" missiles. The pilots aim, fire and then maneuver away to safety while the weapon travels on toward the target.

COMMUNICATION REVOLUTION

Perhaps the greatest revolution in military affairs has been the communications and computer technology used to command modern fighting forces. The U.S. Army and Air Force have been at the cutting edge of this technology. They use modified passenger airliners equipped with radars to monitor events on the battlefield as they happen. Named E-8 JSTARS, these aircraft were used for the first time in the

A Russian Mi-24 attack helicopter fires a missile during an exercise. Helicopters such as this are often used as the first wave of an attack by ground forces.

Personnel Carriers

Modern armies boast a wide range of armored vehicles to support their tank fleets. Infantry fighting vehicles, such as the U.S. Bradley, British Warrior, and Russian BMP, are designed to carry a squad of eight to ten soldiers into battle along with the tanks. These vehicles are almost as mobile and well protected as tanks, but they have smaller weapons designed to deal with threats at a close range, such as enemy trenches or bunkers, and allow troops to leave the vehicle safely. Despite the immense power of tanks, infantry troops follow them closely to clear pockets of resistance from bunkers and buildings. On modern battlefields, engineers and other support teams also follow the action in armored vehicles. They mend damaged vehicles, resupply troops, and help front-line forces navigate around obstacles, cross rivers, and clear minefields.

Persian Gulf War (1991) and gave U.S. commanders a high-altitude view of the battlefield. When linked by high-speed radio links to ground and air forces, the JSTARS allowed U.S. commanders to track and then attack Iraqi troops many miles behind the front line with pin-point accuracy. One example of the power of the JSTARS occurred in the final days of this conflict, when a convoy of Iraqi vehicles was spotted leaving Kuwait. Within a few minutes Allied commanders had ordered their aircraft to attack individual targets in the convoy. Several thousand retreating troops died in the attack on what became known as the "Highway of Death."

DIGITAL BATTLES

Since then the development of digital communications means almost every vehicle and soldier on the battlefield can talk to each other and exchange images and other digital information. This allows commanders to see where every single one of their tanks or troops are on the battlefield on a computer screen in high-tech command posts.

These systems help avoid so-called "friendly fire," in which forces mistakenly attack their own side. In most recent conflicts, a large number of the casualties suffered by U.S. forces and their allies were victims of friendly fire. To avoid friendly fire, troops rely on commanders to direct them.

While these developments offer huge potential to commanders, they also make high-tech forces very vulnerable to jamming or computer viruses that render their equipment useless. Satellite navigation equipment, for example, can easily be jammed with the correct device. In addition, radio transmissions between soldiers could be used to target them.

While the U.S. Army and other armed forces have embraced this technology, most of the world's soldiers are trained and equipped to fight with only the most basic of tactics that have changed little in recent decades. This fact will make it increasingly harder for high- and low-tech soldiers to work together in the future.

A French soldier watches the movements of an entire battle group of tanks and fighting vehicles on a computer screen in a mobile command center.

MASS DESTRUCTION

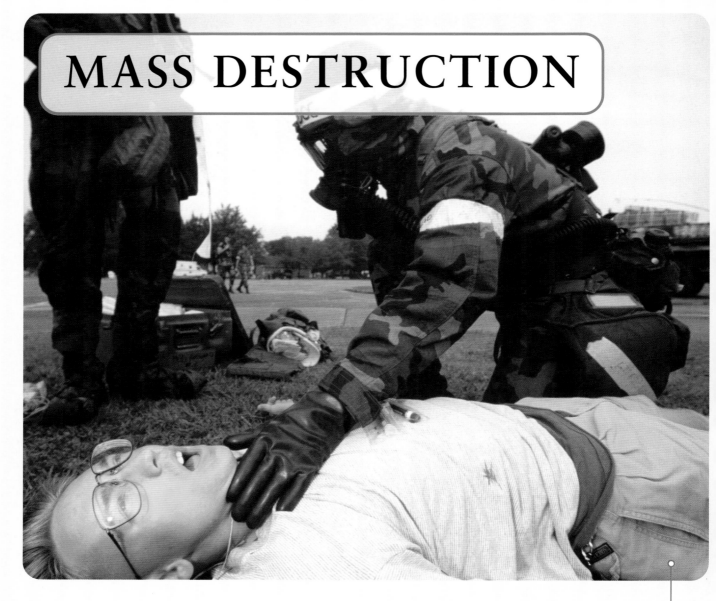

U.S. Marines train to deal with a terrorist nerve-gas attack during a military exercise. A soldier in protective clothing checks to see if one "victim" is still breathing. As well as chemical and biological weapons, there are fears that terrorists might also one day use radiological bombs. These are normal explosives that spread radioactive material over a wide area.

Chemical and biological weapons are described as "poor man's nuclear bombs" because they are less expensive but can still inflict enormous casualties. Along with nuclear weapons, they are known as weapons of mass destruction.

Chemical weapons were first used during World War I (1914–18). Although they were not used during World War II (1939–45), major advances were made in chemical weapons. The first nerve agents were developed at this time. These gases attack a victim's nervous system, causing serious illness or sudden death. Research was also carried out into how highly infectious diseases, such as plague or anthrax, spread, and whether they could be used as weapons to kill or debilitate enemy forces. Despite there being biological agents that could be used to kill large numbers of enemy, they have never been used.

In the Cold War, huge amounts of weapons of mass destruction were stockpiled by both the Soviet Union and United States. As well as building nuclear arsenals, each side also carried on developing chemical and biological weapons. Chemical weapons were designed to knock out large targets, such as airbases and sea ports. They were to be carried in shells, missiles, bombs, or simply sprayed into the wind.

The superpowers never used their weapons of mass destruction, but other leaders did put them into action with devastating effects. When Iraq invaded Iran in 1980, Saddam Hussein (born 1937), the Iraqi leader, thought he would be able to conquer Iran's oilfields. However, Iran fought back, and when it began to threaten Iraq's territory, the United States and other governments gave support to Iraq in order to prevent Iran (then a vocal enemy) from winning the war. Among the things supplied to Iraq were the means to make chemical and biological weapons, such as mustard gas and Sarin and VX nerve agents. Iraq used mustard gas on enemy troops, dropping it from helicopters or firing it from artillery guns. In 1988, Sarin gas was used to kill thousands of civilians in northern Iraq.

When Iraq went to war with United Nations forces in the Persian Gulf War in 1991 these weapons were not used. However, once defeated, Iraq was ordered to destroy all its weapons of mass destruction by the United Nations. A 1993 treaty made chemical and biological weapons illegal. After years of resisting disarmament, the United States and Britain invaded Iraq to overthrow Hussein and destroy any weapons.

Military personnel, such as this U.S. Navy crew member, are equipped with special clothing and masks to protect them against chemical, biological, or nuclear attack. Armed forces have detection devices that give an early warning of such attacks. Those who are affected by the weapons are washed clean and treated with antidotes.

WAR AT SEA

The modern warship has its origins in the Mediterranean Sea about 4,000 years ago when early civilizations, such as the Minoans of Crete, began to use them to protect their territory and trade.

A navy's role has not changed since those early days. It displays military power to enemies, carries troops to foreign shores, and keeps them supplied while fighting far from home. While doing this, warships must also be able to defend themselves from attack by other navies.

CALM WATERS
Although early cargo vessels were generally powered by sail, the most effective naval vessels were galleys powered by oarsmen. Although galleys often had small sails as well, their oars freed them from reliance on the wind and allowed fleets to carry on maneuvering even when the wind dropped in the middle of a battle. Galleys were not armed with many long-range weapons but were often fitted with iron rams on their bows. Most sea battles involved ships ramming each other at high speed in the hope that they would hole the enemy vessel. Failing that, the galley crews, often numbering more than 100, fought with hand weapons.

In the calm Mediterranean Sea, naval galleys ruled the waves for hundreds of years, but they were

A modern destroyer fires a surface-to-air missile to defend itself against an aircraft during an exercise. The ship is also equipped with a helicopter, that lands on a pad at the back.

far from land. The navies of Britain, Spain, Holland, Portugal, and France became the world's dominant sea powers.

For the next 400 years, the main naval weapon was the ship of the line. This ship had several decks, each armed with banks of cannons. The cannons were fired through port holes in the side of the ship. The heaviest cannons were positioned lower down in the ship to prevent the vessel from being too top-heavy and capsizing. There was always a danger that water would pour through the portholes in rough weather, making the ship unstable.

Greek and Persian galleys clash in 480 B.C.E. Sailors fight with hand weapons once their ships get close enough.

much less effective in the windier and rougher conditions of the ocean. Over the centuries sail-powered ships were developed to deal with the rough conditions. By the 15th century, these ships were robust enough to make journeys

IRON AND STEAM

The age of sail was brought to an end in the middle of the 19th century by steamships. These vessels were much faster and more maneuverable. With steam power,

Victory

This ship was the flagship of the Royal Navy at the beginning of the 19th century.

1. Captain and officers lived in cabins in the stern.

2. Lookouts watched the horizon from the foretop.

3. Crew climbed up masts on rope rigging.

4. Cannons were fired through portholes. These were closed during storms.

1

2

3

4

USS **Saint Louise the first American ironclad patrols Union-controlled waters in 1862.**

came iron armor, and "ironclads" —warships plated in metal—were almost invincible to attack by cannonballs. The first ironclads powered by steam were used in action during the American Civil War (1861–65). Dubbed "monitors," these vessels floated low in the water making them hard to spot. Many had huge cannons installed inside rotating turrets. In a series of swift battles, monitors on both sides showed their supremacy over sail-powered and wooden warships. The monitors, however, were only suited to fight in calm inland waters, and were not well suited to rougher waters out at sea.

In 1906, the British Royal Navy began to build a fleet of mighty battleships that could fight in even the roughest seas. These ships were nicknamed *dreadnoughts* after the first to

be launched. They were driven by huge coal-powered steam engines. This made them as fast as any other ship sailing at the time, despite having thickly armored steel hulls and being armed with huge 12-inch (30-cm) guns fitted into rotating turrets. These guns were by far the most powerful weapons on the ocean.

As soon as the first battleship was launched in 1906, it made every other type of warship vulnerable. A "naval race" between Britain and Germany began as each side built bigger and better battleships in the buildup to World War I (1914–18).

The two countries' huge naval fleets fought only once during World War I, at the Battle of Jutland in 1915, when the two navies met off the coast of Denmark. The battle ended inconclusively, with neither side landing a knock-out blow against the other. The Germans were able to hit and damage more British ships, but their fleet could not break out into the North Atlantic. The German warships spent the rest of the war in port and ended up surrendering and being sunk by the British in 1918.

U-BOATS

With its battleship fleet stuck in port, the German Navy turned to submarines or *U-boats* to attack enemy supply ships. A rash of submarine attacks starved Britain of essential equipment and almost forced them to surrender in 1917. The British began to group their supply ships in convoys, which were protected by warships. These tactics reduced British naval losses and ensured vital war supplies got through.

CARRIER GROUPS

During the period between the wars, navies recognized that long-range aircraft would transform naval warfare. The United States, Britain, and Japan began to develop ships that could carry and launch aircraft. These aircraft carriers would be used to launch fighter and bomber attacks from the sea, making it possible to take air forces to anywhere they were needed.

A dramatic air attack on the Italian naval fleet in Taranto harbor in 1940 by British carrier-borne aircraft showed that the battleship was no longer the most powerful sea weapons system. A few months later another carrier attack sunk the German battleship *Bismarck*. These naval battles were the first of their kind, in which aircraft carriers could attack

HMS Dreadnought the world's first battleship sets sail in 1906. This mighty iron ship and others like it were the world's most powerful naval weapons systems for the first half of the 20th century.

Silent Warships

Naval vessels that operated underwater were first used successfully during the American Civil War, but they were very unreliable and difficult to use. By the early 20th century, however, most European navies had fleets of ocean-going submarines, which proved very effective raiders against merchant shipping during the world wars.

The U.S. Navy developed nuclear-powered submarines, and by 1958 one of them had sailed under the polar ice cap. Installing nuclear missiles into naval submarines turned them into the ultimate Cold War deterrence weapon. The U.S. Navy's first missile-carrying submarine, or boomer, was launched in 1960. Subs like this (right) carry the nuclear deterrents of the United States, Britain, France, and Russia, and spend long tours hidden deep beneath the waves. All sides deployed other vessels to defend against enemy submarines. The main weapons in this invisible war were the so-called attack boats or hunter-killer subs that protected the larger boomers.

enemy ships many miles away without having to get within range of enemy guns.

Several months later, the Japanese navy showed the power of its carriers by launching a devastating surprise attack on the U.S. Pacific Fleet anchored in Pearl Harbor, Hawaii, in December 1941. This attack brought the United States into World War II.

The U.S. Navy was well prepared with aircraft carriers of their own, and over the next few months these ships hunted down and sunk most of the Japanese carrier fleet at the battles of Coral Sea and Midway. By 1945, U.S. aircraft carriers dominated the Pacific, destroying what remained of the Japanese navy and supporting the invasion of occupied islands.

UNDERWATER WAR

Submarine technology advanced considerably during World War II. Snorkels were added, so subs could get fresh air without having to come back to the surface. This invention initially gave German U-boats a key advantage during the battle for control of the Atlantic Ocean, in which they attacked supply convoys traveling from the United States to Britain and the Soviet Union.

In response the Allied navies developed new antisubmarine technologies. These included sonar systems, which detect underwater objects, including submarines, by listening for echoes of sound pulses. Radar sets carried on long-range patrol aircraft were also used to detect submarines snorkeling just below the surface.

The nuclear age transformed submarine warfare. As well as carrying nuclear weapons, many modern submarines are powered by small nuclear reactors. Equipped with this supply of power, modern submarines can theoretically stay submerged for many months, even years, since the air inside is recycled using chemical filters. In reality, the subs return to port every few months to change crews and stock up on supplies.

Nuclear submarines are modern dreadnoughts, cruising the world's oceans and almost invulnerable to attack. Their power was first demonstrated in 1982 when a British nuclear-powered attack submarine sunk an Argentinean warship off the Falkland Islands. For the rest of that conflict, the Argentinean fleet remained in port and never threatened the British ships as they landed troops to retake the islands.

NEW ROLES

The end of the Cold War has seen navies develop new weapons for their changing roles. Attack submarines have been rearmed with cruise missiles. They can remain unseen for months on end, lurking close to an enemy coast, and then strike against targets far inland at a moment's notice.

Naval forces are currently being reorganized to defend against attacks by long-range missiles carrying nuclear warheads or other weapons of mass destruction. Because they can cruise close to enemy coasts, air-defense warships can scan for missile launches with their radars and have a good chance of shooting down the weapons before they leave the atmosphere. The remains of any intercepted missiles will then fall back to enemy territory rather than over friendly areas.

To deal with the new demands on the world's navies, warships are being completely redesigned. The Swedish and U.S. navies have launched stealth ships, which are shaped to be invisible to enemy radar. The U.S. Navy is also currently building more destroyers designed to bombard targets on land with cruise missiles.

★ Fact Attack subs use torpedoes to destroy the enemy. Torpedoes are self-propelled bombs that travel underwater. They explode on impact and can home in on the sound of engines.

SUPERCARRIER

At 98,000 tons (88,000 metric tons) the U.S. Navy's Nimitz class aircraft carriers are the largest warships ever to sail the world's oceans. The U.S. Navy describes them as "four and one half acres of sovereign territory." Unlike shore-based aircraft, a carrier's aircraft fly from international waters so they can be launched into action whenever and wherever they are needed.

Supercarriers have immense capabilities. The ships each cost $4.5 billion to build and hundreds of millions of dollars

communication and radar antennae

The superstructure, or "island," is where the ship is controlled and activity on the flight deck is organized.

elevator

patrol aircraft

Catapults launch aircraft down the runway.

take-off runway

Landing aircraft are slowed by arresting wires across the runway.

landing runway

attack aircraft

a year to keep in service. They carry about 80 combat aircraft and helicopters, and a crew of 5,700, including more than 500 women. Each ship is powered by two nuclear reactors, which drive the

Aircraft are stored, loaded, and maintained in a vast hangar under the flight deck. The aircrafts' wings fold up to take up less space. Planes travel between the two decks on huge elevators.

four propellers that push the vessel through the water at 40 mph (64 km/h).

The first U.S. Navy nuclear-powered supercarrier, the USS *Enterprise* was launched in 1960, and since then similar vessels have remained an essential part of U.S. defense ever since. Each carrier is escorted by a battle group of five or six smaller warships and submarines armed with cruise missiles. With their combined naval and air power, a carrier battle group can control a vast area of ocean and protect or attack forces far inland.

Supercarriers and their battle groups are at sea for six months at a time. During this time they are resupplied by support ships so they do not have to put into port until it is time to head home. Although they do not need to refuel during a cruise, nuclear-powered carriers need to be continuously resupplied with food and weapons.

Until 1994, only the U.S. Navy used nuclear-powered supercarriers. In that year France launched its only supercarrier, *Charles de Gaulle*, which carries 40 aircraft. Because of the huge costs involved in building and maintaining nuclear-powered warships, other nations use smaller oil-powered aircraft carriers.

AIR WAR

Air power in the early 21st century is at the heart of modern warfare. During the first one hundred years of powered flight, it has been the needs of the military that have driven most of the advances in aviation.

With the exception of stealth planes, the majority of combat aircraft in service today were designed in the 1960s and 1970s. However, most have been extensively upgraded to allow them to use new generations of accurate guided weapons—so-called "smart bombs."

With their small, swept-back wings, dart-shaped military aircraft are designed to be very fast and highly maneuverable.

However, they have had to sacrifice a lot of their stability to achieve this. The only way modern fighters can stay up in the air is for a computer to control them. This "fly-by-wire" technology relies on information coming from sensors all over the aircraft to keep it flying straight and level. When the pilot changes the plane's direction, he or she is not physically moving the aircraft's control surfaces. Instead it is the computer that calculates how to move the aircraft through a turn.

AIRCRAFT ROLES
Controlling air space is the task of high-flying fighters, such as the U.S. F-15C Eagle, French Mirage

Two F-15 Eagles on patrol. They are armed with heat-seeking missiles, attached to the underside of the wings. The missiles are designed to fly into the engines of enemy aircraft.

2000, Russian Sukhoi Su-27 Flanker, and British Tornado F3. Today, many of these fighters are equipped with long-range sights that can be used to target missiles at other aircraft more than 25 miles away (40 km) away, well beyond the range of the naked eye. Most modern warplanes, such as the F-16 Fighting Falcon, are capable of performing several roles, from controlling the skies to attacking targets on the ground.

There are two roles that still require specialized aircraft, however. The EA-6B Prowler performs the vital role of

Stealth Aircraft

Key inventions

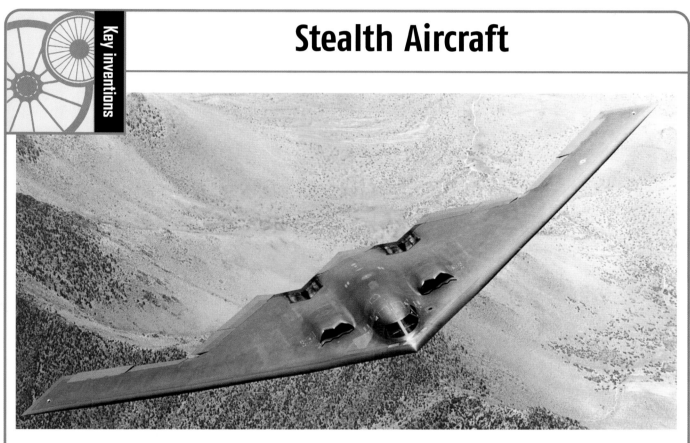

The most expensive aircraft ever built is the bat-wing-shaped B-2 Spirit stealth bomber (above), which cost the U.S. taxpayers $500 million each to buy. A fleet of 21 B-2s were bought by the U.S. Air Force during the 1990s, and they first saw action in the 1999 Kosovo conflict. Subsequently, B-2s were used to spearhead the U.S. air assault on Afghanistan in 2001 and on Iraq in 2003.

The B-2's distinctive shape and radar-absorbent coating are designed to make the aircraft invisible to enemy radar, allowing it to penetrate deep into an enemy's airspace even when the air defenses are working properly. B-2s are armed with satellite-guided bombs, so they can hit targets with pinpoint accuracy in all weathers and even at night. The small size of the B-2 fleet and its cost ensure that the aircraft are saved for only the most important targets.

Smaller stealth aircraft, such as the delta-winged F-117 Nighthawk, first saw action in the 1989 Panama campaign and made the first strike on Baghdad during the Persian Gulf War in 1991. The F-117's stealth design works in a very different way, with the fuselage shaped with many flat faces to reflect radar signals in a random pattern to confuse enemy air defenses.

1   **2**   **3**   **4**   **2**   **5**

A-10 Thunderbolt

Thunderbolts are often in the thick of the fighting. They are designed to keep the pilot safe.

1. Wings are shaped for slow flight over targets.

2. Thunderbolt is armed with a nose gun and missiles under the wings

3. Pilot sits inside heavily armored cockpit.

4. Fuel is stored in several tanks so plane keeps flying if one is punctured.

5. The engines are on the outside of the fuselage, so the plane can keep flying if one is blown off.

suppressing an enemy's air defenses. They are equipped with powerful jammers that send out pulses of radio waves that interfere with enemy radar signals. This has the effect of blinding the enemy so they cannot see the approach of attacking aircraft, and prevents guided-missile defenses from shooting them down.

Dropping bombs close to where your own troops are fighting on the battlefield takes great skill and requires specialist aircraft and highly trained pilots. Aircraft such as the A-10 Thunderbolt and AV-8B Harrier are designed to fly slowly at low altitude over the battlefield and dodge enemy fire before hitting targets, such as

tanks, with pinpoint accuracy. These "tank busters" are designed to fight alongside infantry troops. They have devices on board that can receive information about targets sent up to the plane by troops on the ground.

KEEPING CONTROL
In the Persian Gulf War (1991) more than 2,000 aircraft were airborne each day over Iraq and Kuwait. This required a huge command and control system to make sure they attacked the right targets, kept clear of enemy aircraft, and did not accidentally fly into each other or attack their own side. Missions were all controlled by a central planning

system—the Air Tasking Order (ATO)—in which the details of every aircraft's activities were recorded. The ATO reduced friendly-fire incidents while allowing commanders to make the most of the aircraft available.

Once aircraft take off to attack their targets, it is the job of the E-3 Sentry Airborne Early Warning and Control System (AWACS) aircraft to orchestrate all the different aircraft involved. These aircraft have powerful radars that can monitor thousands of square miles of airspace, identifying all friendly and hostile aircraft. Controllers onboard the AWACS can then reorder the attack plan if something goes wrong or if new targets need to be attacked.

Another key role of the AWACS is to rapidly alert search and rescue teams to spring into action if an aircrew is shot down over enemy territory. Rescue

Robot Planes

How things work

In the long term, many experts believe that combat aircraft in the future will be unpiloted drones. As well as reducing the risk to pilots, drones are less expensive because they have fewer safety systems, and they can make fast maneuvers that would kill or injure a human pilot. Large fleets of drones are already being used for surveillance missions. These include the U.S. Predator and Global Hawk, British Phoenix, and Israeli Hunter aircraft, which are all the size of light aircraft. These aircraft beam live video images of combat zones back to control stations on the ground, so pilots do not have to fly into risky situations. Smaller hand-launched drones, quickly assembled from several components and powered by light electric motors, are also used by ground troops to see behind hills or buildings. Predators (above) have also been armed with Hellfire missiles and used in action over Afghanistan, Iraq, and Yemen. The Predator, however, has limitations because it must always be controlled by a "pilot" on the ground. Drones that can fly by themselves are being developed.

helicopters, such as the MH-53J Pave Low helicopter, are crewed by highly trained special forces, who have night-vision equipment to allow them to operate at night as easily as during the day.

AIR LIFTERS

Moving troops to distant war zones on combat, peacekeeping, or humanitarian missions is a key role for the world's air forces, and they have a wide range of specialist transport aircraft to do the job. The work horse of the world's military air transport fleets is the C-130 Hercules, which can carry 20 tons (18 metric tons) of cargo into rough airstrips or drop up to 50 paratroopers. It has a large rear ramp to allow vehicles to be driven directly into and out off its cargo bay.

The Hercules' big brother is the C-5 Galaxy, which can carry 120 tons (108 metric tons) of cargo including even the largest battle tanks. The C-5 is used to airlift large units but is not risked in small airfields in the combat zone.

In between the C-5 and the C-130 is the C-17 Globemaster, which entered service in the mid-1990s. It can carry 76 tons (68 metric tons) and many of the outsized cargoes carried by the C-5. The smaller C-17 is very maneuverable and can take its chances in some of the more dangerous landing strips.

A helicopter is unloaded from the hold of a C-5 Galaxy. Unlike other airlifters, which unload from the back, the C-5's nose lifts up to open the hold.

Fighters of the Future

As the aging fleets of fighters bought in the 1980s at the height of the Cold War near retirement age, a new generation of combat jets is beginning to emerge from aircraft factories. The U.S. Air Force is taking delivery of its first F-22 Raptor air-supremacy fighters (above) that boast a stealth design and the ability to fly at beyond the speed of sound. In Europe, the French-made Rafale and the Eurofighter Typhoon, made by several European companies, are also starting to enter service. Although not as stealthy as the F-22, they cost half as much as the U.S. aircraft.

The next generation of combat aircraft is likely to be based on the F-35 Joint Strike Fighter. This aircraft has just entered development and will begin active service around 2010. It uses a stealth design and can be fitted with engines suitable for vertical takeoffs and landings.

AIR STRIKE

The last decade of the 20th century saw precision-guided, or "smart," weapons come of age. The video images of laser-guided bombs finding their targets during the 1991 Persian Gulf War convinced politicians that these weapons could transform warfare and dramatically reduce the number of innocent people killed by accident.

The laser-guided weapons used in 1991 were developed from systems first used by U.S. forces in the Vietnam War (1946–1975) during the early 1970s. These bombs were fitted with movable fins and a computerized unit that could detect lasers. The bomb had to be dropped so it traveled toward its target. It then picked up a laser light reflected off the target. The computer gave instructions to the fins to make small adjustments to the bomb's path and make sure it landed on the target. Although inexpensive and relatively reliable, laser-guided bomb kits suffered from a major disadvantage. The pilot had to watch the target at all times to make sure the bomb was locked on. If the pilot had to

take evasive action to avoid enemy defenses or a cloud obscured his view, the bomb would often miss.

One obvious solution to this problem was to use satellites to guide the bomb. The Global Positioning System (GPS) satellites used for this purpose are the same ones that also guide civilian yachts and airliners. They broadcast

An F/A-18 Hornet releases its load of 1000-pound (450-kg) bombs during an exercise. Until recently most bombs were "dumb." They just fell to the ground, destroying whatever they landed on. Most bombs used in warfare today are "smart" and can be guided to a specific target.

a constant stream of radio signals that allow receiving units to calculate their position to within several feet. Satellite-guided bombs have a GPS receiver instead of a laser unit, but they are still flown by small fins. The accuracy is greater than with lasers and it means that GPS bombs, such as the Joint Direct Attack Munitions (JDAMs) used by the United States will work in all weathers and at night. They also allow the pilot of an attacking aircraft to take evasive action immediately after he or she has released the weapon.

While the guidance of smart munitions has improved dramatically, bombs are still very destructive weapons and can kill anyone nearby. Modern bombs are designed to destroy just the minimum amount of a target to take it out of action and avoid unnecessary casualties. The U.S. Navy, for example, has developed warheads for its cruise missiles that release fine carbon fiber cables designed to fuse electricity generating substations. These damage an opponent's power grid, but allow it to be repaired easily at a later date. Concrete warheads have also been fitted to bombs. These smash targets without the need for a massive explosion.

Guidance Systems

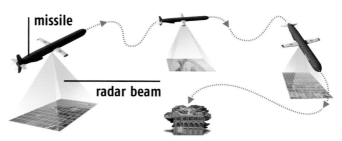

1) A cruise missile uses radar to detect the landscape it is flying over. A computer on board compares this information with a map stored in its memory and flies the missile to the target.

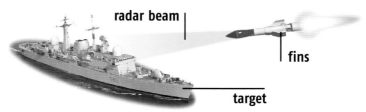

2) An onboard radar in the missile detects the target, and winglike fins steer the bomb toward it.

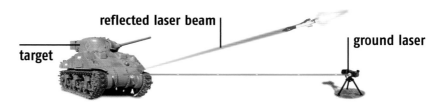

3) A ground force bounces a laser beam off a target. A bomb dropped from a plane flies toward the reflection.

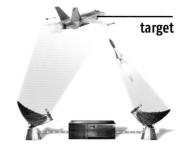

4) One radar detects the target while another follows the missile. A computer steers the missile toward the moving target.

After an air strike, planes return to check that the target has been destroyed. They take pictures of the damage (left).

WAR IN SPACE

An artist's impression of a "Star Wars" system proposed in the 1980s. Missiles launched from the surface would be destroyed by powerful lasers fired from orbiting satellites. This technology was never developed, but the "Star Wars" program has now been replaced with a simpler missile defense system.

The V-2 campaign in World War II (1939–45) was the first military use of space as the German missiles traveled through space before reaching their target. It was not until the Soviets launched their *Sputnik 1* satellite in 1957, however, that space itself became a battleground. The United States immediately ramped up its efforts to dominate this new frontier, and soon it had launched its own satellites. Over the next decade, the United States and the Soviet Union raced to put the first people into space and land on the moon. Each side scored victories in this very public competition. The Soviets, for example, put the first person into orbit around Earth in 1963, but the United States used all its technological might to land a human crew on the Moon in 1969. However, behind the scenes a top secret space race was raging that was to change the way wars were fought for ever.

SPY SATELLITES

Until one of its spy planes was shot down over Russia in 1960, the United States had relied on piloted aircraft to take detailed photographs of their enemy's military bases. Since they could no longer fly into Soviet air space, the United States decided to spy on them from outer space instead.

While NASA, the U.S. space agency, was publicly developing rockets for human space travel, it was secretly launching a fleet of spy satellites into orbit. By the late 1960s, almost all U.S. photographic intelligence was provided by satellites. The first spy satellites had to drop film canisters back to Earth for processing. Once these canisters fell through the atmosphere, they were caught in midair by air force planes. Today, images are sent as coded signals to receivers on the surface. The cameras on the latest satellites produce images clear enough to see individual people.

Photographic spy satellites were soon joined by spacecraft that eavesdrop on enemy communications, and radar satellites that track ships at sea and map the ground very precisely. Many spy satellites have a supply of fuel so they can change orbit to pass over areas of interest.

Space Weapons

At the height of the Cold War, the United States and Soviet Union agreed not to place weapons in orbit around Earth. However both side used space for observation, navigation, and communications, and their satellites soon became potential targets for anyone considering a crippling blow against the many countries that rely on them.

Satellites are sensitive craft and there are several ways of damaging them. A nuclear warhead exploded at high altitude would release a pulse of radiation that damages the delicate electronics inside satellites. Other methods include launching jamming satellites, which would be placed in orbit near key satellites to disrupt the radio signals they send or receive. So-called "killer satellites" fly into orbit alongside the target satellite and explode. The current generation of satellites is not armored so only a small quantity of explosive would be necessary to damage one or push it out of position. Most damage would be caused not by any blast in the vacuum of space, but by high-speed impacts with fragments of metal.

INFORMATION SYSTEM

One of the most important aspects of the U.S. military space program has been the Global Positioning System (GPS) navigation satellites. These were launched in the early 1980s to guide nuclear missiles to their targets. These satellites form a "constellation" in the sky with at least some of the satellites being "visible" to GPS receiver units at all times. The receiver compares signals from several satellites to calculate its precise location. Military units with GPS equipment have a huge advantage over opponents who are relying on more basic navigation methods. GPS signals are also used by civilians, such as for in-car navigation systems. However, civilian receivers cannot decode the signal from the satellites fully, so they are less accurate than military equipment.

The U.S. military has also been in the forefront in using space for communications purposes. It has launched a constellation of specialist satellites to allow its forces based around the world to communicate easily with commanders back in the United States. These include broadband data links that allow commanders to share information or watch live video images transmitted directly from the battlefield. Small handheld radios bounce signals off satellites so troops in remote locations can communicate with their home base. Because their signal travels by satellite, these radios avoid many of the problems

A soldier uses a handheld GPS unit to map an area of Bosnia. The GPS unit is receiving signals from satellites at different points in the sky.

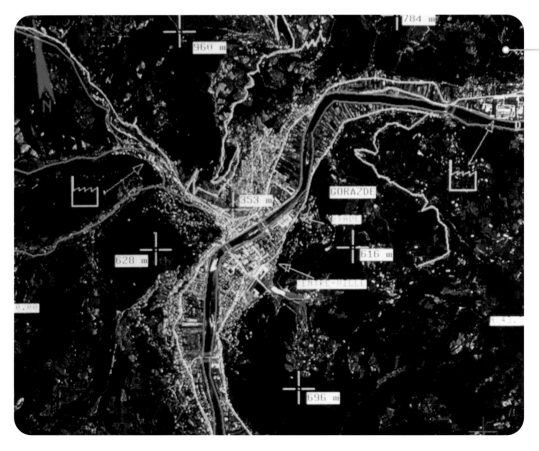

The Bosnian city of Gorazde seen from a French spy satellite. The image is being used to plan an air strike.

Key inventions

Missile Defense

In 1983. U.S. president Ronald Reagan announced his proposal to build a missile-defense system or Strategic Defense Initiative (SDI) to protect the United Sates from attack by Soviet nuclear missiles. Dubbed "Star Wars" by its many critics, this space program made very little progress before the Soviet Union collapsed in 1991, and the threat subsided. The Star Wars concept involved using thousands of weapons based in space, on land, or on ships to

intercept and destroy incoming warheads. A constellation of satellites was to provide an early warning of missile launches.

Missile Busters

In the 1991 Persian Gulf War, Iraq fired missiles at enemy bases and at Israeli cities. The U.S. forces used Patriot missiles to destroy these incoming missiles. But the Patriots did not work very well, and weapons engineers became interested in developing more effective missile defenses. The next time Iraq fired missiles at U.S. forces during the 2003 Iraq War, the Patriot batteries were much more effective.

The United States is also developing defenses against long-range missiles fired by enemy states as a nuclear or chemical-weapon attack. Because these "rogue states" could only be expected to fire a few missiles at a time, this missile defense system had a better chance of success that the earlier Star Wars program.

In 2002, the U.S. government announced that it was withdrawing from the Anti-Ballistic Missile (ABM) Treaty signed by them and the former Soviet Union. This treaty banned the United States from developing missile defenses. As tests continue with varying success (above left), the first base for interceptor missiles is to be located in Alaska to defend against North Korean missiles. Other bases will extend the shield across the country.

suffered by conventional radio systems, such as mountain ranges blocking the signal.

The Soviet Union launched its own equivalent to the GPS constellation but it fell into disrepair as the Communist empire collapsed. The European Union is now proposing to establish its own satellite navigation system. They fear that the U.S. military

might stop access to the GPS system in times of war, crippling many civilian applications.

Because GPS is used in so many military applications, it is useful to be able to disrupt the satellite signal during battles. GPS jammers are now available to protect targets from GPS-guided bombs. They divert the bombs from their intended flight path.

FUTURE WAR

While the high-technology weapons of the United States and its allies provided them with military supremacy during the 1990s, the attacks on Washington, D.C., and New York City on September 11, 2001, showed how small and less well-equipped forces could cause enormous damage. Experts believe that this so-called asymmetric warfare—when a large regular force is opposed by a very small, hard-to-locate irregular one—is set to be a common feature of future wars.

Over the centuries, advances in military technology have soon been superseded by new advances. Few nations have been able to maintain their supremacy in military technology or tactics for long before rivals develop better weapons or countermeasures.

Opponents of the United States looked for ways to attack that did not require them to directly challenge the powerful U.S. armed forces. Hijacking airliners and using them as flying bombs totally surprised the U.S. spy networks and left the country's air defenses almost powerless.

MASS DESTRUCTION
Another way for low-tech units to strike at high-tech forces is by using weapons of mass destruction. Old-style blister agents, such as mustard gas, and biological weapons, such as anthrax, could

Firefighters search for survivors in the ruins of the World Trade Center. The attack that destroyed the world-famous "twin towers" in 2001 was the largest act of terrorism ever, killing nearly 3,000 people.

produce huge casualties and terrorize people. Because these simple weapons are relatively easy to manufacture and release, they are likely to remain a constant threat. New biological weapons are also expected to be created by genetic engineering, probably making existing diseases resistant to drug treatments.

To fight back against these low-tech threats, the United States continues to look for high-tech defenses. One area of current military research is into robotic drones that can deal with threats that would be too dangerous for human operatives. The U.S. Army has launched its massive Future Combat System (FCS) program, which aims to create ground forces that can call on the services of a whole family of

drone vehicles. These will conduct scouting missions in enemy territory or contaminated areas. Naval forces are also developing robots that would protect their ships and subs. Swarms of drones could swim around vessels looking for mines and other threats.

ASSYMETRIC BATTLES

Nations are finding that the main threats they face no longer come from another country's armed forces, but from organized crime gangs and terrorist groups. Military forces alone are not enough to defend against these threats. Police and intelligence agencies must also work to track down the people concerned.

In the future, tanks, fighter aircraft, and nuclear submarines will not be able to tackle these

In October 2001, an unknown terrorist began sending anthrax spores in the mail. The Senate Leader at the time, Tom Daschle, received a letter containing white powdered spores, as did other political leaders, journalists, and law-enforcement officers. Although none of the intended victims died from anthrax, several mail workers who handled the letters were killed.

4TH GRADE
GREENDALE SCHOOL
FRANKLIN PARK NJ 08852

SENATOR DASCHLE
509 HART SENATE OFFICE
BUILDING
WASHINGTON D.C. 20510

20510/4103

small but deadly threats. Armed forces are being restructured to be more mobile as well as connected to global intelligence networks to fight these future conflicts. Arming spy vehicles with guided weapons reduces the time between sensing the enemy and shooting at them. The aim is to knock out enemy forces while they are still preparing to strike.

E-WARFARE

Computer networks and Internet links are likely to be a new realm of warfare as rival armies, terrorist forces, and intelligence agencies try to take control of this vital aspect of modern life. As well as simply destroying an opponent's ability to communicate, future warfare will also involve hacking into the enemy's computer networks. Once inside, enemies could steal vital information and plant computer viruses that would disrupt systems in ways that might not be initially recognized as a hostile attack.

The U.S. military and intelligence service is preparing to defend itself against cyberspace attacks, which could disrupt vital military services and leave them unable to coordinate their military forces effectively. Civilian society is also at risk of cyber-warfare strikes. These would disrupt a whole range of vital services and damage the economy. The U.S. government has now declared that such an attack would constitute an "act of war," and they would respond with force. This obviously presupposes that the culprits could be identified.

A Palestinian boy throws a stone at an Israeli tank. Palestinian fighters and terrorists have been locked in an assymetric war with the Israeli Defense Force for more than 30 years.

The Use of Terror

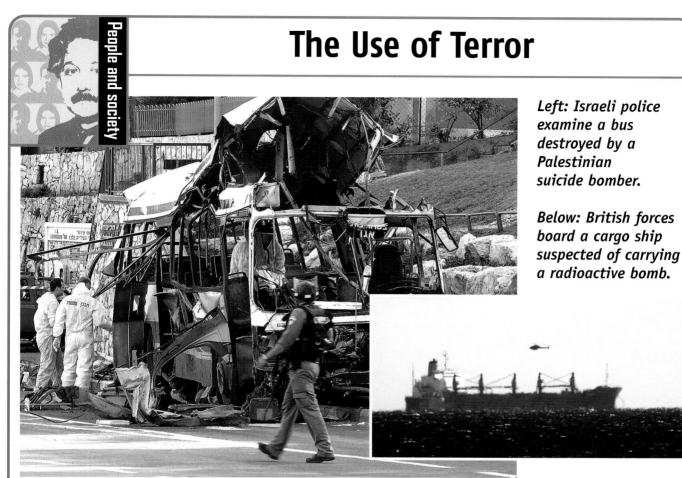

Left: Israeli police examine a bus destroyed by a Palestinian suicide bomber.

Below: British forces board a cargo ship suspected of carrying a radioactive bomb.

Terrorism or using violence to bring about political change is not a new tactic. Also described as guerrilla, or unconventional warfare, this type of conflict pits small groups, or cells, of fighters against conventional security forces and armies.

To achieve their aims, terrorists or guerrillas adopt a wide range of tactics. Ambushes, assassinations, and random attacks on civilians that make normal life impossible are standard guerrilla activities. Attacks are often planned to be so horrific that they result in an overreaction from security forces. This retaliation eventually boosts the support for the terrorists' cause. While they and their supporters call themselves freedom fighters, those on the receiving end of terrorist attacks regard them as criminals.

Guerrilla warfare has been practiced for centuries. The Roman Empire, for example, was often subject to guerrilla attacks, such as from *Zealots*, militant Jewish fighters who rebelled around the first century B.C.E. Ever since then, weaker forces have turned to unconventional warfare to defeat more powerful enemies. The name *guerrilla* fighter was first used during the Napoleonic wars when Spanish peasants rose in revolt against French occupying forces. In the 20th century, revolutionary fighters used guerrilla tactics successfully to take control of countries across the world from Chile to China. Radical Palestinian and European groups specialized in hijacking aircraft in the 1960s and 1970s. In the 1980s and 1990s, Islamic groups began a campaign of suicide bombings against Israeli and Western targets in the Middle East and Africa.

In the future, terrorists might use weapons of mass destruction or attack financial centers. The fear of future attacks is just as damaging as the attacks, since they force governments to reduce personal freedom and increase security.

 Fact Before the 9/11 attacks, the worst U.S. terrorist event was carried out by Timothy McVeigh. He killed 168 people in 1995 by bombing the Federal Building in Oklahoma City.

Time Line

700 B.C.E
Trireme warships
invented in
ancient Athens.

1836
Revolver patented
by Sam Colt.

1916
British use tank in
World War I.

1161 C.E.
Chinese use
explosives
in battle.

1863
First U.S.
submarine launched.

1903
First crewed flight,
by Wright brothers.

700 B.C.E   1100   1900

1864
Nitroglycerine
invented by
Alfred Nobel.

1915
Poison gas used
by Germans in
World War I.

1346
First combat use
of artillery at
Battle of Crecy
in France.

1906
Dreadnought is launched.

1941
First air-launched torpedo attack on warships at Taranto, Italy, during World War II.

1991
U.S. Patriot missiles intercept Iraqi Scud ballistic missiles.

1960
Ballistic-missile-firing submarine launched in United States.

1944
First jet-powered aircraft, German Me 262, sees action.

1999
U.S. Air Force drops first satellite guided bomb in combat in Kosovo.

1949
Soviets explode atom bomb.

1940

1990

1945
Atomic bombs used on Japan.

1958
United States launches first nuclear-powered submarine.

2003
United States uses radio broadcasts to influence the enemy during Iraq War.

1957
Soviet Union launches *Sputnik* satellite.

Glossary

AWACS Airborne Early Warning and Control System, an aircraft that controls the traffic of warplanes

ABM Anti-Ballistic Missile Treaty, an agreement between the United States and Soviet Union to control the number of nuclear weapons.

critical mass The amount of radioactive material that is heavy enough to start a nuclear-fission explosion.

flank A ground force's side.

GPS Global Position Satellite, a navigations system that can pinpoint any position on Earth to within a few feet.

ICBM Intercontinental Ballistic Missile, a weapon that is fired through space to hit anywhere on the surface of Earth.

JDAM Joint Direct Attack Munition, a smart bomb that can fly to its target after being dropped by an aircraft.

JSF Joint Strike Fighter, a new type of warplane.

Mutual Assured Destruction The doctrine that underlies the use of huge arsenals of nuclear weapons as deterrents.

MRV Multiple Re-entry Vehicles, individual warheads carried inside an ICBM.

NORAD North American Air Defense Command, the U.S. military organization that provides early warnings of attacks.

phalanx An infantry formation used by soldiers in ancient Greece.

saltpeter Potassium nitrate, a chemical used in gunpowder.

sarin A chemical weapon that attacks a person's nerves.

SAC Strategic Air Command, the U.S. Air Force body that controlled the fleet of nuclear-armed body during the Cold War.

SDI Strategic Defense Initiative, or Star Wars, a proposed system of space weapons that were to protect the United States from attack by ICBMs.

UAV An unmanned aerial vehicle.

VX A chemical weapon that attacks a person's nerves.

Further Resources

Books

Weapons: An International Encyclopedia from 5000 B.C. to 2000 A.D. by the Diagram Group. St. Martin's Press, 1991.

An Historical Guide to Arms and Armor by Stephen Bull. Checkmark Books, 1991.

Web Sites

Global Security
http://www.globalsecurity.org/

Smithsonian: Military and War
http://www.si.edu/history_and_culture/military_and_war/

USAF Museum
http://www.wpafb.af.mil/museum/

U.S. Army Museums
http://www.army.mil/cmh-pg/Museums/museums.htm

U.S. Navy Museums
http://www.history.navy.mil/

Imperial War Museum, UK
http://www.iwm.org.uk/

Index

Picture Credits

Boeing: 79; **Corbis**: 16, 23, 77, 86, Archivo Iconografico, S.A. 18t; Bettmann 12, 24/25b, 29b, 43, 67t, Gianni Dagli Orti 6, Christel Gerstenberg 34, George Hall 72, 76; Historical Picture Archive 11, Leif Skoogfors 64, 84t, Underwood & Underwood 28; **Defense Image Digest**: 54b, 57, 59t, 59c, 59b; **Defense Visual Information Center**: 82; **DOD Image Collection**: 56, 58, 62, 74, 78, 81; **Mary Evans Picture Library**: 9, 17, 20, 24, 24, 25t; **National Archives**: 2, 26, 30, 44, 68; **PA Photos**: 88, 89; **Rex Features**: 87, SIPA Press 89t; **Robert Hunt Library**: 18b, 32, 33, 35t, 35b, 37, 38, 41, 42, 48, 54t; **Science & Society**: Science Museum 7t, 29t; **Skyscan**: 53, 61; **Sylvia Cordaiy Photo Library**: 7b, 10, 15, 49, 67b, 73; **Topham**: 45, British Library 8, 21; **TRH Pictures**: 27, 36, 40, 47, 51, 52, 60, 63, 66, 69, 70, 75, 84b, Imperial War Museum 39, USAF 50; **U.S. Navy**: Photographer's 3rd mate Heather Hess 65, Vernon Pugh 80; **U.S. Department of Defense**: 85